James W. Moore

At the End of the Day

How Will You Be Remembered?

DIMENSIONS
FOR LIVING

NASHVILLE

AT THE END OF THE DAY
HOW WILL YOU BE REMEMBERED?

Copyright © 2002 by Dimensions for Living

This book is printed on acid-free paper.

Library of Congress Cataloging-in-Publication Data

Moore, James W. (James Wendell), 1938-
  At the end of the day : how will you be remembered? / James W. Moore.
     p. cm.
  ISBN 0-687-04513-4 (pbk. : alk. paper)
  1. Christian life—Methodist authors. I. Title.
  BV4501.3 .M655 2002
  248.4—dc21

                                                          2002004254

Scripture quotations, unless otherwise noted, are from the New Revised Standard Version of the Bible, copyright © 1989, by the Division of Christian Education of the National Council of the Churches of Christ in the United States of America. Used by permission.

Those noted RSV are from the Revised Standard Version of the Bible, copyright © 1946, 1952, 1971 by the Division of Christian Education of the National Council of the Churches of Christ in the United States of America. Used by permission.

Those noted JBP are from The New Testament in Modern English, rev. ed., trans. J. B. Phillips (New York: Macmillan Publishing Co., 1973).

ISBN 978-0-687-04513-6

07 08 09 10 11 — 10 9 8 7 6

MANUFACTURED IN THE UNITED STATES OF AMERICA

For

Daniel Martin Moore

Contents

Introduction

At the End of the Day

When your days on this earth are completed, how will you be remembered? When all is said and done—in the final analysis, "at the end of the day"—what will be your lasting legacy? When people think back over the full spectrum of your life, what will be the most obvious memories of you that will immediately jump into their minds? If your family and friends and acquaintances tried to sum up your life in one word or one phrase, what would that word or phrase be?

When I, as a pastor, sit down with a grief-stricken family to plan the funeral for a loved one who has died, I usually do two things that I have found to be very therapeutic for the family. First, we talk through the details of the memorial service, and second, I ask the family to reminisce with me about their loved one, to think back over the scope of that person's life, and to lift up and say aloud that person's top qualities or attributes.

It's an amazing experience to watch and hear a family do that. They will cry; they will laugh; they will sum up their loved one's life in a word or a phrase, or in a single sentence.

"*Kindness* . . . that's the word; she was just so kind to everyone."

"*Family* . . . it has to be family. She was so devoted to her family, so proud of her family."

"*Caregiver* . . . that says it all. She gave her life taking care of others."

"*Gentleman* . . . he was such a gentleman. Whoever coined the word *gentleman* must have had someone like him in mind."

"*Sense of humor* . . . he was so witty and so fun. He never took himself too seriously. He could light up the room with his humor."

"*Churchman* . . . he loved the church so much."

As I go through this poignant experience with a family, I am always so touched and inspired, and I find myself wondering what words or phrases my family and friends would use to sum up my life when my days on this earth are completed.

I have found that most of the time, people are kind and gracious and thoughtful in their remembering; but this was not always the case. In earlier days, the remembering was done for all to see on tombstones—sometimes with humor and often with amazingly blunt candor. For example, below is a list of actual epitaphs on tombstones from earlier generations.

On the grave of Ezekiel Aikle in Nova Scotia, we find these words:

Here lies Ezekiel Aikle
Age 102
The Good Die Young

In a Ribbesford, England, cemetery, we find this inscription on a tombstone:

Anna Wallace . . .
The children of Israel
Wanted bread
And the Lord sent
Them manna
Old clerk Wallace
Wanted a sweet wife
And the Devil sent him Anna.

In 1837, in Winslow, Maine, somebody was unhappy with a man named Beza Wood, and here's the epitaph on his tombstone:

In memory of Beza Wood
Departed this life November 2, 1837
Aged 45 years
Here lies one Wood
Enclosed in wood
One Wood within another;
The outer wood is very good
We cannot praise the other.

In a cemetery in England, we find this poem:

Remember me as you walk by,
As you are now, so once was I,
As I am now, so shall you be,
Remember this and follow me.

Someone wrote a reply on the tombstone:

To follow you I am not content
Until I know which way you went.

On a tombstone in Georgia are these words:

I told you I was sick.

In a Thurmont, Maryland, cemetery, a tombstone has these blunt words:

Here lies an Atheist
All dressed up
And no place to go.

In a church near Cambridge, England, an Anglican priest is buried with this extraordinary plaque marking his grave:

Here lies Father William who served as vicar of this church for more than 30 years without the slightest trace of enthusiasm.

Well, what do you think? At the end of the day, what will people say about you? If they were totally candid, totally honest, how would your epitaph read? In the Talmud, it is suggested that to be successful in this life, you should plant a tree, have a child, or write a book. This is not to be taken in a strict, literal sense. What it means is this: At the end of the day, be sure you have done something that will be here after you're gone, something that outlasts you; be sure that you have exerted an influence for good in this life that lives on long after your days here are done.

Interestingly, the apostle Paul wrote his own epitaph. In 2 Timothy 4:6-8, we find these powerful words:

As for me, I am already being poured out as a libation [a drink offering to God], and the time of my departure has come. I have fought the good fight, I have finished the race, I have kept the faith. From now on there is reserved for me the crown of righteousness.

Many scholars believe that this was Paul's last letter, written just a few days before he was executed by Nero—a tender moment when he realized that his days on this earth were coming to an end. Reflecting on his life, he wrote these touching words to express his confidence in God, to reassure his friends, and to summarize his life in one sentence: "I have fought the good fight, I have finished the race, I have kept the faith."

So, the question for us is this: At the end of the day, how will *we* be remembered? How will our lives be summed up? And, more pointedly, how well would our lives on this earth measure up to the apostle Paul's three-point formula for living? Let me be more specific by inviting you to think honestly about these three thoughts.

First of All, at the End of the Day, Will You Be Remembered as One Who Fought the Good Fight?

The word *fight* in the original Greek was *agon,* which gives us our word agony. Here, it means "I have given my all. I have stood tall for righteousness and goodness." It's the picture of an athlete leaving the field after having given a total and complete effort, physically drained, but knowing he has given his best, he has given his all. Paul was saying: "All that I am and all that I have, I have given to Christ and to his service; I have fought the good fight."

Introduction ᘛ

Many years ago, there was a movie called *Stars in My Crown*. It is the story of an older African American man who was a devout Christian. He owned a little farm outside a small southern town. Some precious metal was discovered on his property, and great pressure was brought upon him to sell the farm. But he refused to sell because he wanted to stay on the farm that his family had homesteaded. It was his home, and it had been the home of his parents and his grandparents. People, however, would not take no for an answer; they wanted to take advantage of him and cash in on the valuable resources on his farm. So they did everything they could to make him move. They criticized him openly and harshly. They burned down his barn. They shot bullets through his house. Eventually, they threatened to hang him at sundown.

A Methodist minister in the community heard about this and went to visit the older gentleman. While the minister was there, men from the town came out carrying blazing torches and wearing white hoods. The older man stepped out on the porch to face the mob. He was wearing his best clothes, the clothes he wore to church every Sunday. He said he was ready to die and that he had asked the minister to draw up his last will and testament. He then asked the minister to read his will aloud.

As the minister read the will, the mob was stunned because the older man was going to give everything he had to them. He willed the farm to the banker who seemed determined to get it from him any way he could. He gave his rifle to one of the white-hooded men in the crowd who happened to be the man who learned to hunt with this older man. To another, he gave his fishing rod. He literally gave everything he owned to those who wanted to kill him.

The impact on the mob was incredible. Seeing all this goodness and love given in the face of such hate and self-ishness was more than they could stand. In shame and guilt and embarrassment, the men, one by one, turned away and went home, and in time, the entire lynch mob had disappeared.

While all this was happening, the grandson of the minister (who had come out to the farm with him) had been standing to the side of the porch, watching all of this with great curiosity. When the crowd left, he ran over to where his grandfather and the African American man were standing, and he said, "What kind of will was that?" The minister said, "That, my son, was the Will of God."

Indeed so! The will of God is for us to stand tall for what is good and right, but to do it in the spirit of love and grace, and to do it in the spirit of Christ. That's what it means to fight the good fight. The apostle Paul knew that Nero's "lynch mob" would be coming for him very soon, so he put on his clothes of righteousness and said, "Bring 'em on. I'm ready for anything, for Christ is my strength. It's okay. There is reserved for me a crown of righteousness in heaven. All that I am and all that I have, I have given to Christ and to his service; I have fought the good fight!"

Now, let me ask you something. Will you be able to say that at the end of the day? Will you be able to say, with the apostle Paul, "I have given my all for Christ. I have fought the good fight"?

Second, at the End of the Day, Will You Be Remembered as One Who Finished the Race?

Paul said, "I have finished the race." Nobody can understand and appreciate that comment more than a marathon runner. There are several joggers in our church family, and a few of them have become marathon runners. They run over twenty-six miles in those marathon races, along with hundreds of other runners. Of course, every marathon race has a winner, but far more important to the dedicated marathon runner is completing the race.

A friend of ours recently traveled to New England to run for the first time in the famed Boston Marathon. She had no illusions of winning over the hundreds of other runners, but you cannot imagine the joy she felt in finishing the race. She did it. She made it. She ran the entire course. She completed the Boston Marathon, and she could not have been more elated. She finished the race.

The Christian life is like that. It is not a competition to outrun or outdo everybody else. It is a commitment to keep on running even when it's hard, to run all the way to the finish line.

Some years ago, a woman who had been a committed Christian for many years was seriously injured in a car wreck. The next morning, the doctors came into her hospital room and said, "We hate to tell you this, but we are going to have to remove your right eye. It is so badly damaged that we will have to take it out and replace it with an artificial eye." They did not know how the woman would respond to this news. I love what she said: "If you've got to give me a new eye, give me one with a twinkle in it!"

Isn't that great? She didn't quit. She didn't give up. She didn't fall into self-pity. She kept running the Christian race even when it was hard.

That's what she did. That is what the apostle Paul did, and that is precisely what we as Christians are called to do. But the question is, at the end of the day, how will you and I be remembered? Will we be remembered as ones who fought the good fight and as ones who finished the race?

Third and Finally, at the End of the Day, Will You Be Remembered as One Who Kept the Faith?

Some time ago, I visited a good friend. He is approaching ninety years of age, and, as he said it, he will soon be "ninety years young." He is one of the kindest and most gracious persons I have ever known. But at the same time, he has a tenacious sense of commitment: He has been totally committed to his wife for more than sixty years, totally committed to his family, totally committed to Christ and the church, and totally committed to living life to the full.

Word had come to me that this man's legs had given out and that he would not be able to walk anymore. I went out to minister to him, and he ministered to me. I was inspired by his response to his new challenge. When I arrived at his home, he was learning how to operate his new motorized wheelchair. He waved me over and said, "Look at this, Jim. For almost ninety years I have been able to walk around and enjoy the beauties and wonders of God's creation. Blessed be the name of the Lord. Now, they tell me

I can't walk anymore. But look at this: I've got wheels! Blessed be the name of the Lord."

With that, he pushed that lever forward and started driving his chair around the room, laughing and waving and throwing kisses to everybody. That is total commitment—commitment with no strings attached, commitment with no conditions, commitment that keeps on believing even when times are tough, commitment that keeps the faith even when life knocks your legs out from under you.

Let me ask you something. Do you have a tenacious faith like that? At the end of the day, how will you be remembered? Will the world remember you as one who fought the good fight and finished the race and kept the faith?

—◌ 1 ◌—
Will You Be Remembered . . .

As One Who Knew Christ's Healing Love?

Scripture: Acts 3:1-10

A highway patrolman was driving down an interstate highway one morning when he noticed a potentially dangerous situation. A small black car was driving down the highway at a very slow speed. In fact, the car was moving so slowly that other cars were slamming on their brakes and swerving to get around it. The highway patrolman pulled the slow-moving car over.

When the patrolman walked up to the car he had stopped, he found a car full of nuns. He said to the nun who was driving: "Do you know why I stopped you?"

"I have no idea," said the nun. "Was I doing something wrong?"

"Well," said the patrolman, "you were driving so slowly that it was dangerous."

The nun said, "I kept seeing all these signs with the number 20 on them. I figured that was the speed limit, so I was going exactly 20 miles per hour." "No, no, Sister," the highway patrolman said, "that's the *highway* sign, not the speed limit. This is Interstate 20, and the speed limit here is 65 miles per hour, not 20."

Just then, the patrolman glanced in the backseat and noticed that the nuns seated back there had a look of stark terror on their faces, a panic-stricken expression, and their knuckles white from holding onto one another so tightly. The patrolman said to the driving nun, "Pardon me for asking, but what's wrong with the nuns in the backseat?" And the driver said, "I don't know, they've been that way ever since we got off Highway 101 a few miles back!"

Many people go through life like that—riding in the backseat, frozen in fear, and following the lead of someone who may be taking them on a dangerous journey because that leader is reading the signs all wrong!

That is precisely what happened to the man in the third chapter of Acts. The leaders of his society had completely misread the signs, and consequently they had told him, "There is no hope for you. You are under the judgment of God. You cannot walk because you or your parents sinned a great sin, and now God is paying you back, and you'll be this way for the rest of your life. We'd like to help you, but we can't tamper with the justice of God. You can go on down to the Temple gate and beg, and maybe somebody will come by and have pity on you and toss you a coin or two. Sorry, but that's the best we can do for the likes of you." Wasn't that a terrible thing to say to that man? But society in that day had no time for a disenfranchised man. And yet, that is exactly how the leaders of his society treated him, day in and day out in so many ways.

But you and I know that they had misread the signs terribly. They had said to him: "There is no hope for you!

This is your destiny, so just accept it!" But then one afternoon, along came Peter and John, and they said to him: "It
doesn't have to be this way. By the power of Jesus Christ,
you can have a new life. We don't have any coins to toss
your way, but we've got something to give you that's a
whole lot better: 'In the name of Jesus Christ of Nazareth,
stand up and walk.'" Then, notice this, the words are fascinating here. The Scriptures say that Peter took the man
by the right hand and "raised him up"; raised him up!
That means he got resurrected!

It was unbelievable. The man discovered that he could
stand on his own two feet, and suddenly he began to do a
jig right there on the Temple steps. The song of resurrection was being played, and he was dancing to the beat!
People came running from all directions. They knew who
this man was. He had been a fixture there for some time.
He had been sitting there begging every day for years.
Someone had always carried him to the Beautiful Gate in
the morning and carried him home each night. And now,
he was jumping up and down like a man possessed. Peter
then said to the crowd that this miracle was done through
the power of the risen Christ. It was faith that made it happen. As the story ends, Peter and John and the healed man
all link arms and go into the Temple together (v. 11). Don't
you know that in that moment, somewhere in heaven,
Jesus was smiling, so glad to see his disciples taking up his
ministry of healing and redemptive love.

What a great story this is! Not just because it describes
a dramatic and wonderful miracle healing that took place
long ago, but even more because it also so powerfully out-
lines what Christ's love can do for you and me right here

and right now. Let me show you what I mean with some thoughts that can serve as a great formula for life for you and me. Are you ready? Here's number one.

First of All, Christ's Healing Love Gives Us a Self We Can Live With

This man's self-esteem needed a shot in the arm. All his life, he had been told not only that he was worthless, but also that God had it in for him. Nothing could be further from the truth, but that was the message his world sent him in words and deeds and attitudes. But then, here came Peter and John to tell him that he counted, that he mattered, that he was important, that he was special, that they valued him, but most important, that God loved him.

Some years ago, there was a priest in New York City named Father Joe. Father Joe entered the priesthood after pursuing several colorful careers. He was a soldier in Vietnam, a professional football player, and a singer in a band that never took off. In his midthirties, he decided to go to seminary and train to be a priest. When he was ordained, he was assigned to a parish in South Bronx.

One day, he got into an argument with a cabdriver who had parked in front of the church. One thing led to another, and suddenly Father Joe forgot the thin veneer of his new profession and grabbed the cabbie, pinning him against a fence. The cabbie reached for his knife, but fortunately other people stepped in and broke it up before anyone got hurt. Father Joe was mortified at what he had done and how he had acted. He knew that this was no way for a priest to behave. He was so ashamed, cut to the heart. It was terrible. A few minutes later he had to say Mass with that ugliness, that hate, that anger rising in him. It hurt to pray. He was confused and embarrassed. What does *love your neighbor* mean? he wondered. He looked up at the cross and knew he had failed. He had not loved his enemy. He had wanted to fight. Father Joe wondered if he was worthy to be a priest.

While he was grappling with his soul, Father Joe had a visitor. Jasmine was her name. Jasmine was a little girl who came by the church every morning to get a glass of milk. Little Jasmine knew nothing of what had happened, but she gave Father Joe something that morning that brought him out of his spiritual crisis. It was a note scribbled with a first-grader's pencil. It read, "Dear Father Joe . . . I love you once, I love you twice, I love you more than beans and rice." That's all, but it was just what Father Joe needed. He read her poem and smiled and understood the larger message, too. Jasmine had reminded him of what's really important. She was an angel that day (a messenger from God). Jasmine reminded him that we are loved and accepted as we are. With all our weaknesses and foibles, God loves us and accepts us just as we are.

That is the message of the Christian faith. Even though we sin, even though we fail, even though we aren't perfect, God doesn't desert us, God doesn't forsake us, and God doesn't give up on us. God still loves us and accepts us, and in so doing, God gives us, by the miracle of his amazing grace, a self we can live with.

Second, Christ's Healing Love Gives Us a Faith We Can Live By

In the fall semester of 1997, two male sophomore students at Duke University were taking Organic Chemistry. They both had done very well on all the quizzes, the midterm exam, and the lab assignments, and both had a solid A going into the final exam. The two friends were so confident about taking the final that instead of studying, they partied the weekend before the final exam, which was scheduled for 8:00 A.M. on Monday. However, they partied so much that they overslept Monday morning and missed their exam.

They went to the professor to explain, and they made up quite a story. They told him that they were out of town for the weekend and planned to come back in plenty of time to study, but they had had a flat tire on the way back and did not have a spare tire. They were stranded on the highway and only just now got back to campus; could they take the final exam at another time? The professor thought this over for a moment and then agreed to let them take the final exam at 8:00 the next morning. The two guys were elated, and they studied organic chemistry all night long.

The next morning, the professor placed them in separate rooms and handed each of them a test booklet and told them to begin. On the first page was written: "Question One (value 5 points): Describe and give a specific illustration of free radical formation."

"Great," they thought, "we know this. This is going to be easy." Each completed that problem and turned to the next page. They were unprepared, however, for what they saw on the page. It said: "Question Two (value 95 points): WHICH TIRE?" (*Homiletics* [July 1998]: 24-25).

They had been caught—"done in." They were brought down by their high-sounding but false words. Like a boomerang, their lie came back to haunt them. There's a lesson there somewhere, and I think it is this: Christianity is not just a creed we profess; it is a lifestyle we live. It's not enough to say the words. We must live our faith in the day-to-day world. One of the things that is so beautiful in this story in Acts 3 is that we see Peter and John living their faith out in the world and sharing their faith with this man in need, giving to him the love of Jesus and the healing that only Christ can bring.

The great artist Rembrandt did a fascinating thing in one of his paintings. Instead of painting a halo over the head of Jesus in one work of art, he painted a halo around his hands. Not over his head, but around his hands! Why? Over the years, art critics have debated why Rembrandt did this. It seems to me that he was reminding us of all the ways Christ used his hands to do his ministry. With his holy and sacred hands, he healed the sick, fed the hungry, blessed the children, and raised the dead. With his hands, he showed us how to live faith and how to put our faith to work. With the sacred touch of his hands, he gives us a self we can live with and a faith we can live by.

Third and Finally, Christ's Healing Love Gives Us a Love We Can Live Out

A little boy in his Sunday school class was asked this question: "Johnny, what do you think the Bible is trying to teach us?" I love Johnny's answer. He said, "The Bible is telling us to love God and to love people 365 days each year, and to be sure not to take too many days off."

In Keith Miller's book *A Second Touch* ([Waco, Tex.: Word Books, 1967], 63-64), there is a story about a busy executive living in an eastern city, who was rushing to catch a train. He had been so caught up in the pressures and hassles and stresses of the business world that he was worn to a frazzle. There were so many demands, so many deadlines. So this day, he rebelled. On this particular morning, he decided really to try to be a Christian instead of just talking about it. This day, no matter what, he was going to live in the spirit of Jesus Christ's love.

Just as he was boarding the train, he accidentally bumped into a little boy who was carrying a jigsaw puzzle. The pieces scattered everywhere. Normally, the man would have jumped on the train and rushed to the office without offering to help the boy, but he remembered his decision to live in the spirit of Christ's love. So he stopped and helped the boy pick up the puzzle pieces. The train started to pull out slowly.

The little boy watched him closely, realizing the sacrifice the man had made and realizing the man had missed his train in order to help. When all the puzzle pieces were found and safely back in the box, the little boy said, "Mister, are you Jesus?"

That's probably what that man at the Temple wanted to ask Peter that day: "Hey, Mister, are you Jesus?"

Now, let me ask you something. Has anyone ever seen the love of Jesus that powerfully in you? My prayer is that God, through the power of the risen Christ and the presence of the Holy Spirit, will enable us to live each day in such a way that when we come to the end of our days on this earth, we will be remembered as persons, who by the healing love of Christ, had a self we could live with, a faith we could live by, and a love we could live out.

Will You Be Remembered . . .

As One Who Celebrated the Joy of the Journey?

Scripture: Deuteronomy 34:1-8

Some years ago, Robert J. Hastings wrote a classic essay called "The Station." In it, he shows us that it is not enough to long for a happy ending somewhere in the distant future, but rather, he reminds us that there is great joy in the journey through life. In powerful and colorful words, Hastings invites us to imagine that our life is like a long, long trip on a passenger train. There is beautiful scenery to see and savor, fascinating people to meet and appreciate. But instead we give our energy to focusing on our final destination. We can't enjoy the trip because we can't wait to make it to the station. Restless, impatient, we pace the aisles and count the minutes and resent the waste of time it takes to make the journey. We long to hurry and make it to the station. All this traveling is so much drudgery. When we finally reach the station, real life will begin.

Hastings translates that to mean that real life will begin when I get that new car, when I finish putting my kids through college, when I get that new job, or when I reach retirement. Then I can really live.

Hastings points out that it doesn't work that way. When we arrive at that destination, we don't find the fulfillment we had so longed for and wanted. Then Hastings says this: "The true joy of life is in the journey! So relish the moment!"

He urges us to stop counting the miles and pacing the aisles and instead to begin seeing each day as a precious gift from God. Rejoice in it and be thankful for it. Celebrate life and see the miracles of God all around us. Live life to the full as we go along. The station will come soon enough.

Is Robert J. Hastings right? What do *you* think? Is it possible that we get so caught up in our dream of a "happy ending" that we miss the joy of the journey? Could it be that we sometimes look so intently for some "promised land" tucked away in the distant future that we become amazingly blind to what we already have at our fingertips? Let's think about this together for a few moments. Very simply, I want to lay a few ideas before you. Here is idea number one.

First, the Truth Is That We All Have Known Some Disappointment, Some Frustration, Some Uncompleted Task, Some Unhappy Ending

All of us have known the experience of wanting some promised land and yet never quite getting there. Let me show you what I mean.

Remember Abraham Lincoln. He led the nation through terrible conflict. He brought the American Civil

War to an end. He was ready to lead our nation in peace, "with malice toward none and charity for all." But it did not turn out that way. He went to Ford's Theatre in Washington D.C. one night and was assassinated. So quickly, so harshly, so abruptly, so tragically, it was over for him. He was so near the promised land, but he only "glimpsed it from afar."

Some years ago, a young left-handed pitcher broke into the major leagues of professional baseball. He was so talented that he quickly made headlines with his scorching fastball. He became an all-star in his rookie season and was destined to become one of the greatest pitchers of all time. However, early in his career, during the off-season, he slipped while mowing his lawn, barefooted. His foot went under the mower and was severely cut. He underwent surgery, and his foot healed. Somehow, the accident affected his stride, and Herb Score's fastball was never the same. In a few short months, he realized that he could not make a comeback, and he dropped out of baseball while still in his early twenties. He was so near the promised land, but he only glimpsed it from afar.

Several months ago, I was asked to conduct the funeral service of a young teacher who had died after just a few years of teaching. His mother was brokenhearted, and she expressed what many must have felt. "It's such a shame! He spent all those years getting ready to do what he wanted more than anything. He wanted to teach, to challenge young minds and influence their lives for good. And now this!" she said. "And now this!"

Or think of the man who dreamed for years of his retirement. All those things he wanted to do and share with his wife, all those places to visit, trips to make, sights to see—but then, when he retired, his wife was stricken with an illness and was slowly wasting away before his very eyes. He, too, could have said it: "All those big dreams, and now this!"

Well, all of this brings us to one of the most moving stories in all the Bible: the story of Moses. Remember Moses. Remember how abruptly his story ends. For forty years, he grappled with a cantankerous people. For forty years, he wandered with them in the wilderness. For forty years, he struggled to hold them in line. For forty years, he was a pilgrim and a sojourner. For forty years, he slept in a nomad's tent under the stars and lived off the land. All to one end: that he might reach the Promised Land! For forty years, he had dreamed of it. But then Moses died before they got there; a stone's throw short of his goal and life-long dream, and he died!

Does this seem unfair? Was it a tragedy? Was Moses' life a failure? Or is it possible that though Moses never reached the land physically, he had been there in his heart and mind and soul all along? You see, the truth is that Moses *had* possessed the promised land all along. He had it in his heart. He had seen it, felt it, dreamed it, lived it, loved it from day one. One ancient legend that has emerged out of this poignant story shows Moses protesting at first. But in the legend, God says to him, "Come on now, Moses. *Why* must you cross over into the Promised Land? You've always had it in your heart. Your people never have. Let them enter. You've been there long enough. Now it is time for you to come home and be with me."

This is a very important lesson to learn, isn't it? That the real promised lands are within us. We don't have to wait. We can claim the promised land now. We can have *heaven* now. Isn't that great? We don't have to wait until we die. Heaven can begin for us now. This is the first idea. It is a fact that in this life we will experience disappointment and have unreached goals. But the good news is that God is with us! This is idea number one.

Second, Happy Endings Are Fine, I'm Sure, but Don't Forget That There Is Great Joy in the Journey

When we spend all our time thinking of and longing for "the sweet by and by," we may miss "the joy of the here and nigh." Let me ask you something. What is failure, anyway? How would *you* define it? Most of us are easily tempted to define *failure* as not arriving where we intended to arrive, not achieving our goals, not meeting our objectives. Well, I'm all in favor of setting goals and having objectives and working toward them. But I certainly don't agree with the tough football coach who said, "Show me a good loser, and I'll show you a loser!"

Come on, now! What about Moses? Moses did not reach his goal. He meant to enter the Promised Land, but he didn't get there. But does that make him a failure? I should say not! What about all those years of commitment and obedience and faithfulness? What about that motley crew of renegade people that he shaped into the servant people of God? What about the impact of his life on human history? Indeed, on your life and mine? What about the loyalty and devotion and character he built?

What about the Ten Commandments he brought down from Mount Sinai? His victory was in the journey!

The author Robert Louis Stevenson had an untimely death. He was only forty-four years old when he died. Some would insist that his journey was too brief—but not Stevenson. He would not say that! He would not complain! He never lost hope. He never gave up. He never quit on life. He never became bitter. Later, facing imminent death, he asked his friends to place on his tombstone these words: "Gladly did I live, and gladly die, and I laid me down with a will."

The *journey* is what counts. When you look at Moses and what happened to him, the point is driven home powerfully. The bigger part of his story was the traveling—*not* the arriving. So the lesson for us is clear: Enjoy the journey! Smell the roses! Celebrate the present. Live in the now moment. Sow the seeds of God's love everywhere you go. Feel God's spirit within you. Claim heaven now—today— and trust God for tomorrow, trust God for the ending.

Third and Finally, Nothing That Is Really Great and Important Is Ever Finished in One Generation

Each person dies with something left undone. We never do all we wanted to do. We never do all we intended to do. We never see all we hoped to see. We never become all we dreamed of becoming. Maybe that's what John Wesley meant when he said, "We are going on to perfection." The journey is our home. The joy is in the pilgrimage. So we have to learn the hard lessons of patience and trust. We must do what we can and then trust other people and God to see that what we have begun will be continued. We do our best and trust God for the rest.

There is a wonderful film entitled *The Lucky Star* (1980). It's about a thirteen-year-old boy who is left behind in Nazi–occupied Holland when his parents are swept away to a World War II death camp. He is a brave, decent, honorable, hopeful, faithful young man—an inspiration to the Dutch villagers. He dreams of freedom. He longs for it. He sings of it. He talks about it. He wants so much to be free! But when his life is threatened by the Nazis, he begins to see that his days are numbered. He begins to see his dream fade, but not his faith, and he speaks wonderful words to those who threatened his life: He says that whether dead or alive, he will win because what he stands for will live on in the town—he stands for freedom.

Those powerful words remind us of our Resurrection faith, of Jesus, and of his journey. He came singing love. He lived singing love. He died singing love. He rose in silence. If the song is to continue, we must do the singing. Now, that is what the Christian journey is about—the sacred privilege and awesome responsibility that is now ours, to "go tell it on the mountain, over the hills and everywhere that Jesus Christ is born," to go tell it on the mountain over the hills and everywhere that the Savior has come into the world.

By the way, do you recall that Jesus lived and taught on the move? He was born on a journey. He died on a journey. He rose again on a journey. And in doing this, he shows us not only that there is great joy in the journey, but also that God is with us every step of the way.

—☙ 3 ❧—
Will You Be Remembered . . .

As One Who Knew the Gift of the Holy Spirit?

Scripture: Acts 2:1-4

I want to share with you a book I picked up recently. It's a humorous little book called *You Might Be a United Methodist If . . .* by United Methodist pastor Robert Martin Walker (St. Louis, Mo.: Chalice Press, 1998). Obviously, it's a take-off on Jeff Foxworthy's stand-up comedy routine "You Might Be a Redneck If . . ." which is simply a series of comical comments such as, "If you have an old, rusted-out car sitting on concrete blocks, draped with a rebel flag, in your front yard, you might be a redneck."

In similar fashion, Walker's book pokes good-natured fun at United Methodists with comments like these:

You know that a circuit rider is not an electrical device.
You think UMW stands for United Methodist Women rather than United Mine Workers.
You realize that *The Book of Discipline* is not a guide for getting your children to behave.
Your congregation's Christmas pageant has both boy and girl wise men.

You've ever owned a pair of cross-and-flame boxer shorts.

And this final one, which leads into the subject matter of this chapter:

You don't take a Rolaids when your heart is strangely warmed.

The great preacher and writer Dr. Leslie Weatherhead once told a wonderful story about his visit to the place where John Wesley, the founder of Methodism, had his famous heart-warming experience at Aldersgate. Unfortunately, the little Aldersgate chapel does not exist anymore. It's long since been torn down. Now, there is just a plaque on the side of a building that marks the spot. But at the time of Leslie Weatherhead's visit, there was still a chapel.

Weatherhead described that experience like this. He said that on the side of one of the pews in the dimly lit chapel was a small plaque with a tiny light over it. The plaque read: "On this spot on May 24, 1738, John Wesley's heart was strangely warmed."

Being there in that special place was a moving moment for Weatherhead, and he wanted to bask in the glow of it for a while, so he sat down on the last pew to think and pray and reflect. Suddenly the door of the chapel opened, and in came an older man with a cane, wearing a heavy and tattered overcoat. The older man, not seeing Leslie Weatherhead in the darkness of the chapel, walked slowly down the center aisle. When he got alongside the John Wesley pew, he noticed the plaque. Curious, he walked over, bent down, and read the words out loud: "On this spot on May 24, 1738, John Wesley's heart was strangely warmed." Immediately, the older man dropped down on his knees, looked upward, and said, "Do it again, Lord! Do it again for me!"

Isn't that a wonderful story? And isn't that a great prayer? "Do it again, Lord. Do it again for me!" Warm my heart! We are not exactly sure what happened to John Wesley at Aldersgate some two hundred and sixty years ago. We certainly could not begin to put it into words. That kind of experience defies description. Words are not adequate to express or capture a spiritual moment like that. But we do know this: That heart-warming experience gave John Wesley a new start, a new life, a new warmth, a new energy, a new purpose, and a new power, and it produced a new church. Somehow, the fire of the Holy Spirit brushed across his heart and set John Wesley aflame!

Did you know that during his ministry, John Wesley rode over 250,000 miles on horseback to preach the Word? That's a quarter of a million miles—a distance roughly equal to ten complete trips around the globe! On a *horse*!

Did you know that John Wesley preached over forty thousand sermons, and that he and his brother, Charles, wrote close to seven thousand hymns?

Did you know that John Wesley invented many cures for diseases, wrote a book on medicine, and started clinics for the poor?

Did you know that at John Wesley's death in 1791, his followers numbered seventy-nine thousand in England and forty thousand in America, but by 1957 there were forty million Methodists worldwide?

Did you know that for all the power of his eyes, his voice, his witness for Christ, John Wesley was only five-feet-three-inches tall and weighed only 128 pounds? This man, small of physical stature, became a spiritual giant. *Why?* Because his heart was strangely warmed, because he received the gift of the Holy Spirit! That is precisely what happened to the disciples of Jesus at Pentecost. Remember that they were powerless before the Holy Spirit came. But when they received the gift of the Holy Spirit, it warmed their hearts, set them aflame, and they turned the world upside down! Justin Wroe Nixon put it like this: "The basic difference between physical [power] and spiritual power is that [we] use physical power but spiritual power uses [us]!" (Wilson Weldon, *Mark the Road* [Nashville: Upper Room, 1973], 85).

We see the Holy Spirit dramatically in the experience of Peter. Relying on his own strength, he failed miserably. Over and over, he said the wrong things at the wrong times. In a panic, he tried the way of the sword. And then in the crunch moment, he denied his Lord three times. But when the Holy Spirit exploded into his life, he got fired up, and he did the best he could and trusted God to bring it out right. And when he preached that day at Pentecost, three thousand souls were saved!

We also see the Holy Spirit graphically in John Wesley. Relying on his own strength, he went to Georgia as a missionary and failed miserably. But then at Aldersgate, his heart was strangely warmed. He realized that God was with him, trusted God, did the best he could, and incredible, miraculous things happened. The writer of Acts was on target when he referred to the Holy Spirit as a "gift" (Acts 2:38). It is indeed a gift from God, a gift that can turn our lives around, that can take our feeble efforts and use them in amazing ways, that can turn our weakness into strength and our defeats into victories. Let me show you what I mean.

First, the Holy Spirit Redeems Situations

The Holy Spirit can take a bad scene and convert it and use it for good. This truth is powerfully portrayed in the experience of Zan Holmes of Dallas. Dr. Holmes is one of the most distinguished preachers of America, and he tells of something that happened to him when he was a first-year seminary student. His church was so proud of him and his call to the ministry. He had been asked by his pastor, Dr. I. B. Loud, to read the Scripture lesson one Sunday morning. Zan read the Scripture and then settled back to listen to the sermon.

But Dr. Loud did something most unusual that morning. He stepped into the pulpit and said how proud everybody was of Zan Holmes and his efforts to become a minister. And he announced that it would be a good idea if "Brother Zan came to the pulpit and delivered the sermon of the morning!" Young Zan Holmes said he nearly died right on the spot! He was terrified as he walked from his chair to the pulpit. He says there are still fingernail marks gouged into the wood of the pulpit where he clutched it for dear life, as he tried frantically to think of something—anything—to say.

Finally, he remembered a sermon that he had been working on for preaching class. His mind raced, and he began to preach that sermon. He says it was pretty good, all three-and-a-half minutes of it. But then he ran out of steam. He felt so alone, so empty, so vulnerable, so defeated as he stood before that anticipating congregation. It was an awful moment because he could not think of anything to say. And Zan Holmes began to cry.

Then he heard the voice of an older woman in the congregation, saying, "Help him, Lord Jesus." Then came the familiar voice of a man from the bass section of the choir. It boomed out, "Come, Holy Spirit." Zan Holmes said he then looked down on the front pew and saw two precious little girls who suddenly began to clap their hands in rhythm and sing the spiritual "Amen." Before long, the entire congregation was clapping and singing, and Zan Holmes said, "I just stood there and watched God work!" Zan learned a valuable lesson that morning: "It is the Holy Spirit who finishes the sermon!"

If we do the best we can, God will do the rest. That's what happened at Pentecost. Peter did his best and let God finish it. He did his best and then stood back and watched God work. God does not ask us to be successful; God only asks us to be faithful. If we give our all, if we do our best, if we genuinely try to do God's will, then God will bring it out right. The Spirit of God can take a weak voice and make it a trumpet. The Spirit can take a defeat and turn it into a victory.

The Holy Spirit can redeem situations! That's a very important thing to know. Now here is a second thought.

Second, the Holy Spirit Reminds Us of the Truth

That's what happened at Pentecost. The Holy Spirit blew on that place and brought God's truth. Throughout the Scriptures, the Holy Spirit is the "Truth giver." The Holy Spirit comes to reveal God's truth.

Dr. Fred Craddock is one of the great teachers of preaching in our country. He tells a moving story about something that happened to him in the early days of his ministry. He was helping with vacation Bible school. He said, "It used to last for two weeks, but there were so many casualties among the teachers that we reduced it to one week!" Fred Craddock said that he had a group of juniors who were "driving him up the wall," especially after ten or eleven days with them, and especially one boy in the class. Dr. Craddock described that difficult boy like this:

> There was this one boy in the class who . . . well, let me put it like this. . . . Have you ever had somebody in class that was so bad that you were glad when they were absent? . . . He was that type! . . . And quite honestly, I had written him off. He's not paying attention, I thought. He doesn't care. He doesn't want to be here. He is not interested in the lessons. He is only interested in seeing how crazy he can drive me and in disrupting the class. He is hopeless!

Dr. Craddock said he had gotten so worn out with it all that he was now simply trying to think of things for the students to do to keep them busy and out of his hair, and he thought of something. He decided to send them outside on a nature study, a study of creation. He gathered them at the door and said, "Now listen, when I ring the bell, I want you all to go outside and scatter and find one of God's miracles. And then when I ring it again, come back and show us what you have and tell what it teaches us about God." Dr. Craddock rang the bell, and they scattered. He said that his plan was "not to ring it again."

But he did. After a while, he rang the bell, and they came back with God's miracles. "Well, what do you have?" Dr. Craddock asked. One young boy had a rock. He said, "This rock reminds us that God is stout and God made the world." One girl had a flower. She said, "Only God could make a flower like this. It's so pretty!" Another girl had a leaf that had fallen off the tree and had turned brown. She said, "God made the seasons of the year, summer, fall, winter, spring." Another boy stepped forward with some huckleberries. He said, "God provides for us. He feeds the animals, and he feeds us."

"Well, that's great," said Dr. Craddock, and then he looked over and saw that especially disruptive boy, standing off to one side, with nothing in his hands. Instead, he was standing there holding the hand of his little sister, who had been down in the kindergarten class. Dr. Craddock was exasperated, and he thought, *What is he doing? Why won't he cooperate? I guess they have to leave early. Why didn't somebody tell me?*

Then this conversation took place.

"Leaving early?"

"No, sir."

"Well, did you bring anything?"

"Yes, sir."

"What did you bring?"

"My little sister!"

"Your little sister?"

"Yes, sir."

"Why did you do that?"

"'Cause she's God's miracle. I prayed for a little sister, and God gave me one. She's the best miracle I know of!"

Dr. Craddock stood there stunned because he knew the little boy was right! And he knew that God was there in that room, in that moment, closer than breathing. Craddock said, "I don't know whatever happened to that boy, but I hope he's still doing that. He was the only one in the class (including the teacher) who got the point." The Holy Spirit touched that little boy's heart when nobody was looking and gave him the truth—the truth that God's greatest miracles are people! "You want to see one of God's miracles? I'll go get my sister!"

This is one of the greatest truths of the Bible. We—you and I—are made in the image of God. Talk about a miracle! God made the squirrels, the elephants, the giraffes, and the duck-billed platypus. God made the trees, the flowers, and the skies. God made all of it and said, "That's good! Now, that's good!" And to cap it all off, God said, "Now, for the masterpiece: I am going to create something like myself!" And God made you! And it is a sin for us to say, "Well, I'm only human." If you want to see one of God's miracles, don't gather the pine cones, don't capture the squirrel, don't find a picture of a trout stream; just look at the person next to you. *There* is God's miracle! There is the crown of God's creation!

Sometimes when we least expect it, the Holy Spirit reveals the truth. That's what happened in that Vacation Bible School classroom that morning. There's another lesson here: Don't ever write anybody off. And whatever you do, don't write off the Holy Spirit. That's what Pentecost teaches us. The Holy Spirit redeems situations. The Holy Spirit reminds us of the truth.

Third and Finally, the Holy Spirit Restores Our Strength

Peter was down, defeated, and embarrassed. He had failed. He had denied his Master at the critical moment. He had seen the Crucifixion and was devastated. He had met the resurrected Christ, but still he felt like a failure. He felt inadequate for the task. But then came the Holy Spirit, and Peter's strength was replenished. Empowered by the Spirit, Peter became a man of courage and a tower of strength! The Holy Spirit restores our strength.

Some members of our church are going through a valley right now. It's one of the toughest situations you can imagine. A few days ago, I went to minister to them, and they ministered to me. They said, "Don't worry about us. We are going to make it. We are taking this one day at a time, and God is with us as never before. He is giving us strength. He will see us through!"

"God is with us as never before. He will see us through"; that is the good news of our faith, isn't it? God never deserts us. He redeems situations for us. He reminds us of the truth. And he restores our strength.

Have you heard the story about a young man who approached the father of his girlfriend to ask his permission to marry her? The father was skeptical. He said, "You don't know what you are asking. She has very extravagant tastes. I doubt very much that you will ever be able to support my daughter. I'm a wealthy man, and I can barely manage it myself." The young man thought for a moment, and then he said, "Sir, I believe I have it: You and I could pool our resources!"

That's the message of the Christian faith, isn't it? We are not alone. God is with us, we can pool our resources with him, and his strength will see us through. God's strength will carry us. God's strength will save us.

So, the question is, How is it with *you?* Have you made that discovery? Will you be remembered at the end of the day as one who knew the gift of the Holy Spirit?

—∞ 4 ∞—
Will You Be Remembered . . .

As One Who Knew How to Trust the Right Things?

Scripture: Joshua 24:14-18

Charles was a graduate of the U.S. Naval Academy. He was a highly respected and much-decorated jet pilot in Vietnam. He flew seventy-five successful combat missions. But on his seventy-sixth mission, his plane was hit and destroyed by a surface-to-air missile. Charles ejected and parachuted to safety. However, he was captured by the enemy and spent some time as a prisoner of war. He did survive the horrible ordeal, and now he goes about the country giving lectures about what he learned from that traumatic experience.

One day, Charles and his wife were sitting in a restaurant. A man at another table saw them and came over and said, "Hey! I remember you! You flew jet fighters in Vietnam from the aircraft carrier *Kitty Hawk!* You were shot down!"

"How in the world did you know that?" Charles asked.

And the man said, "I'm the guy who packed your parachute!" Charles gasped in surprise and in gratitude, and he stood up to shake the man's hand. The man pumped his hand vigorously and said, "I guess it worked."

Charles assured him, "It sure did. If the parachute you packed hadn't worked, I wouldn't be here today."

Charles could not sleep that night. He kept thinking about that man, wondering what he might have looked like in his Navy uniform of a white sailor's cap, a bib in the back, and bell-bottom trousers. Charles wondered how many times he might have seen him on the ship or brushed past him in a narrow corridor without speaking. Because, after all, Charles was a fighter pilot, and he was just a sailor. Charles thought of the many hours that young sailor had spent standing at a long, wooden table on the aircraft carrier, carefully weaving the shrouds and folding the silks of each chute, holding in his hands somebody else's life.

Now, the question that explodes out of this story is this: Who's packing *your* parachute? Who's getting you ready for the crucial moments, the decisive moments, the challenging moments, the crisis moments of life? Who's packing your parachute: Who are you trusting to do that lifesaving job for you? This is one of the single most critical questions in life. In whom or in what do you put your trust?

Everywhere we go, every step we take, there is an incessant clamoring for our trust. From every corner comes the loud screaming or the tempting whispers, "Put your trust in me!" "Put your hope in me!" "Give your allegiance to me!" "You can count on me!" "Let me pack your parachute!"

Money says that. Military might says that. Gangs and cliques say that. Alcohol and drugs say that. Material possessions say that. They all say enticingly: "Put your trust in me." "Put your hope in me." "Give your allegiance to me." "Let me pack your parachute."

I can't stop thinking about the tragic school shooting a few years ago in Littleton, Colorado. Those two teenagers, the shooters, had put their trust in violence and assault weapons, in anger and rage and revenge, but their trust was in the wrong place. The "parachute" did not work, and the result was death and destruction and suffering and heartache and incredible loss for so many. Indescribable, horrific pain was the result for so many because two young men put their trust in the wrong things. Unbelievable agony affected so many because two young men chose wrongly.

Now, this is precisely what the scripture lesson in Joshua 24 is all about. Remember how forcefully Joshua said it: "Choose this day whom you will serve . . . ; but as for me and my household, we will serve the LORD." We will put our trust in God. This is without question one of the greatest statements in all of the Bible.

But what was the context of this? What prompted Joshua to make this great pronouncement? If you listen closely, you can hear strong commitment in his words, and also a tone of exasperation. You see, after all those years of wandering in the wilderness, the Hebrews had now come into the "Promised Land." They had dreamed of this, they had longed for this, and they had prayed for this.

But now that they were in the land, there was a big problem. Other people lived in the land, too, and these other people had their own set of gods that they worshiped. They had a god of war, a god of wine, a god of fertility, and a god of this and that and the other. And some of these false gods apparently were attractive to the Hebrews. In fact, some of these false gods were so enticing to the Hebrews that they actually began worshiping them instead of worshiping the Lord, which, of course, was a blatant violation of the first commandment.

Joshua saw what they were doing, and forcefully, boldly, and dramatically, he said, "Choose this day whom you will serve, whether the gods . . . beyond the River or the gods of the Amorites in whose land you are living; but as for me and my household, we will serve the LORD."

This story in Joshua is about choices, decisions, commitments, and priorities. It is about deciding to whom we will give our allegiance and our loyalty. It is about choosing where we will put our hope and our trust. It is about selecting the packer of our parachute. Now, let me boldly say three things about that—three strong recommendations.

First of All, Put Your Trust in Your Family

Joshua said, "As for me and my household." Family was obviously a priority for him, and it should be for us.

Our granddaughter Sarah is quite a character, highly verbal, and dramatically expressive, and we never know what she is going to say next. A few years ago, when she was five years old, Sarah did an interesting thing with her family.

This particular afternoon she put on her gymnastics costume and then brought her mom, dad, and little brother, Paul, out to the backyard. She arranged three seats for them in front of the swing set, and then she gave her family instructions. She said, "You are the audience, and I am going to perform for you on the swing set. Whenever I do something great, you go *ooh, aah* and applaud; and whenever I do something fantastic, you go *ooh, aah* and applaud and then turn and say to each other, 'Isn't she beautiful?'"

Now, let me say something to parents and to grandparents and to all of us. Some kids do not have the bold spirit that Sarah has. Some kids are not able just to blurt it out like Sarah does, but that's what they want, and that's what they need. They want us to ooh and aah over them. And they want us to think they are beautiful and great.

At a board of stewards meeting a few years ago, we had a discussion about the tragedy in Littleton, Colorado. It was a heart-wrenching discussion about what we can learn from that horrifying event and how we as a church can respond. As we talked, my mind darted back to an article I had read. Syndicated columnist William Raspberry wrote the article, and in it he shared an analogy that is haunting and helpful. He said that "children are our canaries" ("Young Killers Are Taking Cues from Uncivil Adults," *Lexington Herald-Leader,* 24 May 1998). Coal miners would go deep into the mines, and sometimes they would unknowingly move into a dangerous atmosphere, an atmosphere made toxic by methane gas. Some of the miners would be overcome by the dangerous levels of methane gas, and some of them would die.

So, the miners knew that they needed some kind of warning system to alert them to the danger. Here's what they did. They took canaries in cages down into the depths of the mine with them. When the canaries, with their smaller and more sensitive respiratory systems, would begin to gasp for air, the miners would know at that moment that they were breathing poison into their lungs. The gasping canaries would warn them that they were in a toxic atmosphere.

That is precisely what our children do for us. Our children are our canaries. When they turn to violence or profanity or cruelty, they are giving us a warning. They are telling us that we, as a culture, have moved them into a dangerous, poisonous place, a deadly, toxic atmosphere, and we need to get them and everybody else out of there as fast as we can. Let me show you what I mean.

Children today are "gasping" over guns. Where do kids get guns? In most cases, the guns come from their homes or from a friend's home. This is poisonous. We must find ways to limit access to weapons of deadly force.

Children today also are gasping over violence in the entertainment world. They are exposed to way too much violence and way too much profanity on TV and in movies and video games. This is poisonous. We must find ways to convince the entertainment world to change its ways because they are creating a dangerous, toxic atmosphere.

Children today are gasping over bigotry. Any tendency on our part to put down, label, ostracize, marginalize, or alienate anyone because of his or her looks, interests, or skin color is wrong and poisonous. We must find ways to eliminate prejudice.

Children today are gasping over double standards. If we act one way at church on Sunday and another way the rest of the week, we are giving kids the toxic message that what we do in church has little to do with the "real" world.

Children today are also gasping over a culture where many kids are left to raise themselves as mothers and fathers are otherwise occupied. When this happens, who or what becomes the "parent"? Who or what communicates values?

In the board meeting that Wednesday night, one church member said something that touched me. He said he was grateful for his parents because as he grew up, they gave him three things he needed so much: love, discipline, and supervision. He knew they loved him. He knew the rules. He knew they were aware of what he was doing.

That's what all children need, isn't it? Love, discipline, and supervision. They need a strong sense of family. They need to know that even as they take some hard knocks out in the world, at home they are loved and respected and cherished. The parachute for the tough times needs to be packed at home. We need to trust our families, and our families need to be trustworthy.

Second, Put Your Trust in Your Church

I deliberately put these thoughts in this order, the church right beside the family, for this reason. We all know that some children and young people—and indeed, some adults—are not getting what they need at home. If that's the case for any one of you, then come to the church. Let us be your family. Let us give you the love and the discipline and the supervision you need.

I know a young man who had a tough situation at home. His father had deserted the family, and they had not heard from him in years. This young man's mother was doing the best she could, but to make ends meet she had to work two minimum-wage jobs—one during the day and one at night. Consequently she was never home. So, the young man adopted the church, and we adopted him. We became his family. He pretty much lived at the church. He put his trust in the church, and now he is one of the finest young men I know.

Harold Kushner, in his book *Who Needs God?* (New York: Pocket Books, 1989), put it like this:

> What does the church offer that we lonely human souls need? In a word it offers community . . . a refuge, an island of caring in the midst of a hostile, competitive world. In a society that segregates the old from the young, the rich from the poor, the successful from the struggling, . . . the church represents one place where the barriers fall and we all stand equal before God. It promises to be the one place in society where my gain does not have to mean your loss . . . that we can meet people as brothers and sisters, not as buyers and sellers. (P. 103-4)

Ken Medema expresses the need of so many lost and hurting people in his song "If This Is Not a Place." He asks for a place where one can go when seeking answers and acceptance and when needing to speak and be heard. There aren't many places in the world that will accept all as they are, and few will listen. So many people need a place of friendship and love and security, but there aren't many opportunities for these. So where do we go for acceptance and love? Medema sings:

If this is not a place where tears are understood, where can
   I go to cry?
If this is not a place where my spirit takes wing, where can
   I go to fly?

The church is this place of love and growth and acceptance.

"Who's packing your parachute?" Put your trust in
your family and in your church.

Third and Finally, Put Your Trust in God

A wealthy man and his son loved to collect rare works
of art. They had everything in their collection from Picasso
to Monet to Van Gogh to Raphael. They often would sit
together and admire the great works of art.

When the Vietnam War broke out, the son went to war.
He was very courageous and died in battle while rescuing
another soldier. The father was notified, and he grieved
deeply for his only son.

About a month later, there was a knock at the door. A
young man stood there with a large package in his hands.
He said, "Sir, you don't know me, but I am the soldier for
whom your son gave his life. He saved many lives that day,
and he was carrying me to safety when he was hit. We
were close friends, and he often talked to me about you.
He told me about your love for art. I know this isn't much.
I'm not really a great artist, but I want you to have this
painting."

The father opened the package. It was a portrait of his
son, painted by the young man. The father was amazed at

how this young soldier had captured his son's personality in the painting. He offered to pay the young artist. "Oh, no, sir, your son gave his life for me. This is my gift to you." The father hung the painting over his mantel, and when visitors came, he showed them the painting of his son first before showing them any of the other great works of his collection.

A few months later the man died. There was to be a great auction of his paintings. Many people gathered, excited over the possibility of purchasing one of the great works.

The auctioneer first presented the painting of the man's son. "We will start the bidding with this portrait of his son. Who will bid for this picture?" There was silence. Then a voice of protest from the back of the room: "We want to see the famous paintings. Skip this one. Let's get to the good stuff—the Rembrandts, the Raphaels, the Van Goghs, the Monets. Let's get on with the real bids."

But the auctioneer would not bend. "The son! The son! Who'll take the son?" Finally, a voice came from the back of the room. It was the longtime gardener of the man and his son. "I'll give ten dollars for the painting. I loved that boy. Wish I had more to offer."

"We have ten dollars. Who will bid twenty?"

"Oh, just give it to him for ten dollars! Let's get to the masters."

"Ten dollars is the bid. Won't someone bid twenty?" Now the crowd was angry. They didn't want the picture of the son. They wanted the more worthy investments for their collection. The auctioneer pounded the gavel. "Going once . . . twice . . . *sold,* for ten dollars." A man sitting in the second row shouted, "Now, let's get on with the collection!"

The auctioneer laid down his gavel. "Sorry," he said, "the auction is over."

"What about the great paintings?" the crowd demanded.

"I'm sorry. I have my instructions. There was a secret stipulation in the will, which I was not allowed to reveal until this time. Only the painting of the son would be auctioned. Whoever bought the painting would inherit the entire estate, including all the paintings. The man who took the son gets everything!"

That's where to put your trust. God gave his Son two thousand years ago to die for you and me. And much like the auctioneer's call, God's message today is "The Son! The Son! Who'll take the Son?" Whoever takes the Son gets everything!" "Choose this day whom you will serve . . . ; but as for me and my household, we will serve the LORD."

Well, how is it with you right now? Where are you putting your trust? What will people say about you at the end of the day? When your days on this earth are completed and people sit around and reminisce about you, what will they say? What will they remember? Will you be remembered as one who knew how to trust the right things? That is something to think about, isn't it?

5

Will You Be Remembered . . .

As One Who Knew the Power of Compassion?

Scripture: Luke 10:25-37

In November 1955, a little boy wrote an essay that was published in *The West Virginia Hospital News*. The boy's essay was on anatomy and was titled "What Makes Up a Person."

He describes the human body and its parts' functions in a poignant way. He calls the head "round and hard" on which hair grows and in which our brains are. He says the face is "where you eat and make faces." The neck keeps our heads out of our shirt collars, and shoulders are where suspenders are hooked. The stomach hurts when we do not eat properly, and the spine is always behind us. The young boy further explains; arms are for pitching, fingers are for throwing baseballs, and legs are for running. What he describes are the tangible parts of the human body, or what is on the outside. But he ends his essay with this observation: "And that's all there is of you, except what's inside, and I never saw it."

Isn't that great? I hope that young man got an A on his

59

essay. But when he left out "what's inside," the truth is, he left out the most important part. For you see, it's what is inside that really counts! Jesus talked a lot about this. He wanted us to make our lives count for something good, and he believed the key is the inner life—what's inside us. He was deeply concerned about those inner motives that make us tick—our hopes, our dreams, our values, our attitudes, our purposes, and our approach to life.

Remember how the poet illustrates this:

All the water in the world, no matter how hard it tried
Could never ever sink a ship unless it gets inside.

In other words, all of the worries and problems that hang over us and cause us stress will never be able to "sink" or "wreck" us as long as we do not let that stress inside to take over. Because what's inside is so tremendously important!

Jesus knew this, and he once told a story about it, a story that suggests that there are three approaches to life. You can approach life with a cold heart, with a calculating heart, or with a compassionate heart. The story, of course, is the parable of the good Samaritan. You may remember it.

1. A man is beaten and robbed and left seriously injured on the roadside by the robbers, the thieves, and the bandits. They are the coldhearted people. They say, "We want what you've got, and we are big enough to take it away from you!" Some people go through life like that. They are coldhearted takers, grabbers, and robbers. Their attitudes are totally selfish: *What's in it for me, and how can I cheat*

you out of it or beat you out of it? These are the folk who approach life with a "cold heart."

2. Then there are other people like the priest and the Levite who see the injured man. They don't want to get involved, so they nervously tiptoe by on the other side. These are the people who approach life with a "calculating heart."

3. Then there is the Samaritan—the *good* Samaritan. He is "good" because he is compassionate. He is a giver. His approach to life is to do something good and helpful; to do something productive and creative; to do something loving; to bring healing where there is hurt; to go through life with a caring, compassionate heart.

Consider with me this simple outline. These three approaches are possibilities for us. Which type of person are you? Which do you want to be? Which will you be today and tomorrow and all the rest of your life? Will you exhibit a cold heart, a calculating heart, or a compassionate heart? Let's take a look at these, one at a time. We may find ourselves here, somewhere between the lines.

First of All, It Is Possible to Be a Person with a Cold, Cold Heart

That can be your attitude, your basic approach to life. You can have a diminishing, destructive effect upon this world by being a coldhearted taker, a selfish, ruthless person who uses and abuses other people. You can be a grabber, a robber, a thief, and a parasite. You can lurk in the shadows, waiting to pounce on innocent persons, to take advantage of other people, to overpower them and take away what they have. That's the way some people approach life.

About the time Jesus was born in Bethlehem, there was a king in Israel named Herod. Herod was a coldhearted person. He always negotiated from power. He always looked out for number one. In many ways, Herod was a brilliant man: He was a genius at political scheming and intrigue. He was also selfish, sadistic, and cruel. In fact, shortly before he died, Herod decreed that on the day of his death, three hundred prominent citizens in his kingdom should be executed!

Follow his thinking. He knew that Israel would not grieve over his passing. He had been too mean and tyrannical. He knew that the Israelites might dance with joy in the streets over his death. So he came up with a ploy to prevent that from happening and perhaps to deceive history as to his own importance and image. His idea was that if three hundred beloved people were killed on the day he died, there would be a lot of grief in the streets, and history might think that the grief and sorrow were for him. His plan didn't work, of course. Herod died, and the world in which he lived was glad. People like Herod, who are selfish, coldhearted takers, live in every age.

What about you? What impact do you have on the world? Is it constructive or destructive? Is it positive or negative? Do you build up or tear down? Do you give? Or do you take? Do you hurt? Or do you heal? Are you self-centered? or self-giving? Why do people live lives in coldhearted ways that distort and pervert God's intention? I think it has to do with attitudes, with approaches to life.

You see, this coldhearted, selfish approach is not life as God meant it to be. It is not limited to robbers. There are many "respectable people" who take advantage of others, who think only of themselves, who insist on doing things their way without concern for what happens to other people. Recall how the Scriptures describe the robbers: They "stripped him, beat him, and went away, leaving him half dead" (Luke 10:30). I wonder if that has ever been said symbolically about me or about you. I wonder if we have ever, in some way, hurt somebody and left him or her "half dead."

In the "Peanuts" comic strip, Charlie Brown's little sister, Sally, tries to talk Charlie Brown into doing her homework for her. Charlie Brown says to her, "Sally, if I do your homework for you, what will you be learning?" Sally answers, "I'll be learning that all-important lesson in life: How to Manipulate Other People!"

Some people go through life like that—pushing, shoving, grabbing, hurting, robbing, stealing, manipulating, and taking from others. I hope that is not true of us; but it is one possible approach to life. We can choose to be selfish people who approach life with a cold heart.

The Second Possibility Is to Be a Person with a Calculating Heart

This is the person with a scared, nervous, fearful I-don't-want-to-get-involved heart. But the Bible will not let us get away with that. The Bible says to us that it will not work—not really—to be apathetic or lukewarm or calculating; not to be able to decide is to decide to do nothing.

In the book of Revelation, there is a disturbing verse addressed to the church in Laodicea that says, "I know your works; you are neither cold nor hot. . . . So, because you are lukewarm . . . I am about to spit you out of my mouth" (Revelation 3:15-16). Those were perilous days in the life of the church, days when a Christian had to take a stand. And some of the Christians in Laodicea were trying to tiptoe through life, not hurting anybody, but not helping either.

In the good Samaritan parable, the priest and the Levite were calculating tiptoers. Their attitude was "I'm not going to hurt you, but I don't want to be bothered with you. I don't want to get involved in this. After all, it's none of my business. It's too risky. It's none of my affair." So they went by on the other side.

A lot of people come at life like that—nervous, fearful, calculating, indifferent, insensitive, with no compassion for the needs of others. They always anxiously protect their own best interests; they are not cruel, don't hurt other people, but look out for themselves. They walk that shaky tightrope of trying not to get involved in the hurts of other people and excuse themselves by saying, "I'm only one person. What can I do? I am so insignificant. What I do really doesn't matter."

But you see, what I do, and what you do—what *we* do—*does* matter. It matters more than I can say. Let me illustrate. I love music and would like so much to be a good musician. But the truth is that when it comes to music, I'm a challenging case. Some years ago, I decided that I wanted to learn to play the piano and took some lessons, but I think the exposure was harmless. My teacher, an older woman, was so steeped in the great classics that she even closed her eyes when she said the word *music,* and she would put her hand on her heart when she mentioned the name of the great composer Mozart.

As the days went by, I learned to play with Christian charity; in other words, "my left hand didn't know what my right hand was doing"! Finally, one day, I got up the nerve to ask my teacher how I was doing and if she thought I would ever become a good pianist. She was a lady of great tact, and after long thought she said, "Well, it will take a lot of practice, a lot of discipline, a lot of lessons, a lot of hard work, a lot of prayer, and a whole lot of money!" From that point, I began to lose my enthusiasm! But I did learn one thing in my music studies, one very important thing: namely, that every single note is important! Let one key on the piano stick, or let one note be out of tune, and an entire composition can be reduced to shambles. There are no unimportant notes on a piano, and there are no unimportant lives in God's world. God does not expect any one of us to change the whole world single-handedly, but God does expect us to do what we can to improve the little corner where we live.

And my question to you is this: What about *your* influence? Is your city a better place because you live there? Is your church a better church because you are a part of it? Is the tone of your family or workplace Christian and good and beautiful because of your witness and your spirit? It's so important. In the same way that one note on a piano refusing to play can ruin the whole piece, so does our failure to become involved affect the larger melody of God's plan in the world.

We can approach life with a cold heart or with a calculating heart.

The Third Possibility Is That We Can Approach Life with a Compassionate Heart

Our lives can be constructive and productive and creative. We can be peacemakers. We can be people who care, help, love, serve, and act with compassion. We can bring healing where there is hurt.

In the "Peanuts" comic strip, Lucy decides that her brother Linus has to learn to live without his security blanket. So, while he is taking a nap, she steals his blanket, and buries it outside. When Linus wakes up, he misses his blanket immediately. He goes into a claustrophobic panic. He screams, he shouts, he pounds the floor, he gasps for air and cries, "I can't live without my blanket!" And then he faints.

Snoopy, the trusty dog, sees Linus's dilemma and rises to the occasion. He goes outside, sniffs out the blanket, digs it up, and brings it back to Linus. Linus is relieved and ecstatic. With one hand he grabs the blanket, and with the other he grabs Snoopy. He kisses Snoopy and hugs him and pats him and thanks him over and over and over. The last panel shows Snoopy lying on his back on top of his doghouse, thinking this thought: "Every now and then, my existence is justified!" You see, this is the point. Compassion is what it's all about. Loving others and helping others and healing their hurts is the justification for our existence.

Some years ago, the great Henry Van Dyke gave a classic description of the people in the good Samaritan parable. He pointed out that the robbers came, saying, "What's yours is mine, and I'll take it!" The priest and the Levite passed by on the other side, saying, "What's mine is mine, and I'll keep it!" The good Samaritan stopped and helped the man, saying, "What's mine is yours, and let's share it!"

Remember how the Scriptures describe the good Samaritan? Look at these active, verbal expressions: "He was moved with pity (he had compassion)"; "He went to him"; "[He] bandaged his wounds"; "[He] brought him to an inn"; "[He] took care of him"; "He took out [money], gave [it] to the innkeeper, and said, 'Take care of him (Luke 10:33-35).'" Sometimes we get confused about what life really means. But Jesus makes it clear that we are to be compassionate healers.

Let me conclude with some very quick observations about this parable:

1. For one thing, the choice is ours. The point is that we all have within us, at any given moment, the potential to be any one of these three types of people. So, today when you walk out of your home, tomorrow when you go to the breakfast table or to the office or to school, you can be cold, you can be calculating, or you can be compassionate. The choice is yours. It's up to you.

2. Notice too that when Jesus talks about eternal life or our accountability to God, he often ends up talking about love! He often raises the question, "How did you treat your neighbor?" Now, notice something here. Jesus never answers the lawyer's question because the lawyer was asking the wrong question. The question is not "Who is my neighbor?" The question is "Whose neighbor am I?" The

question is not "Who will love me?" The question is "To whom can I reach out with love?"

3. Finally, if you want life—*real and eternal life*—don't be cold, don't be calculating! Be compassionate! Accept Jesus Christ, the Prince of Peace, into your heart and pass on his loving, caring, compassionate spirit to others. You don't have to have a cold heart, and you don't have to have a calculating heart. Jesus can warm your heart and put his compassion deep in your soul.

Jesus is our good Samaritan, and he wants us, in his spirit and by his grace, to be good Samaritans for others. Well, what do you think? How will you be remembered? Will people remember you as one who had a cold heart, a calculating heart, or a compassionate heart?

6

Will You Be Remembered . . .

As One Who Knew How to Teach Children the Key Things in Life?

Scripture: 1 Corinthians 13:1-7

How do we teach our children to be loving people? Let me prime the pump of our thinking with this illustration. My granddaughter Sarah is a delightful personality who is never at a loss for words. When she was six years old, her mother took her to a public playground. Sarah immediately began to play with two other little girls on the playground equipment. The two other girls were three or four years older than Sarah, and they were sisters.

As they were playing, the older sister got upset with her younger sister and said to her with anger, "You are stupid and ugly!" When Sarah heard that, she said, "Word Police! Word Police!" The older girl turned to Sarah and said, "What did you say?" Sarah replied, "I said, 'Word Police.'" The older girl retorted, "Why did you say that?" Sarah answered, "I said 'Word Police' because you said two bad words." "What bad words did I say?" the older girl questioned. Sarah responded, "You said 'stupid' and 'ugly,' and those are bad words; and when you say bad words, the 'Word Police' come out!" "Oh, yeah?" said the older girl, "Well, how about ——— ?" and she blurted out a four-letter word that I would not say anywhere and certainly not in this book. And Sarah said, "Yep! I think *that* would be one, too!"

Now, what is interesting about that true-life experience at that public playground is this: On the one hand, we see that one child is being taught daily how to be loving, gracious, and respectful toward others, and also, how to stand tall for what is right and good. She has learned at home and at church that it is not nice to call someone stupid or ugly. On the other hand, the other child was allowed to say mean words while her parents were sitting right there on a bench within earshot of that colorful conversation. They were reading magazines. They never looked up, never said a word, and never corrected their daughter.

In recent years, psychologists have emphasized strongly how tremendously important those early years are. Our personalities, our attitudes, our values, our habits, our principles, our self-esteem, and even our IQs are shaped by what happens to us in those first few years of early childhood.

Again last summer, we had vacation Bible school. It was a great experience. The quote of the week came from one of our four-year-olds, who said, "I like Bible school at St. Luke's better than Thanksgiving, Valentine's, and Chuck E. Cheese pizza!" Now, *that's* saying something!

In one Bible school resource, there was a poem that touched my heart. It was called "A Child's Appeal." It was written by Mamie Gene Cole and uses a child's voice to speak to the world. This child says, "Here I am, the one you've waited for. I'm the one who will decide what tomorrow's world will be. But I don't know anything about the world yet. I don't understand why I'm here or how I got here, but I want to know why and how. So help me, encourage me, and teach me what I need to know, because what you teach me will determine who I will become." The poem ends with these words:

> Give me, I pray you, those things that make for happiness.
> Train me, I beg you, that I may be a blessing to the world.

How do we *do* that? How do we train our children that they may be a blessing to the world? How do we crown their heads with wisdom and fill their hearts with love and set them on the right paths? What are the best things we can do for—and give to—our children?

Not long ago, a fourteen-year-old girl was suspended from school for cheating. When her mother tried to talk to her about it, the girl screamed, "So what? Everything's different now. We don't go by your rules anymore!" "I guess that's true," the shaken mother said to me later, "and I don't know how to cope with it."

Well, *is* that true? Can it be that in this troubled, stressful, hectic, fast-changing, pressure-packed world in which we live, the rules have changed? Have the values changed so that we don't know what to teach our children anymore? Do we just improvise as we go along? Of course not! Of *course* not! No matter how fast times may change, no matter how much customs may change, certain qualities always abide, certain values always endure, certain truths are always relevant, certain attitudes are always appropriate, and certain actions are always right.

What are these enduring values? I have thought about this for a long time and could not begin to list them all, but here are a few to try on for size. I'm sure you will think of others.

First of All, There Is Honesty

The apostle Paul put it like this: "Love does not rejoice in what is wrong; it rejoices in what is right" (paraphrase of RSV). We need to teach our children that integrity matters, that honesty is so important! Nothing will ever change the need for honesty. In fact, it is impossible to imagine any livable society without it. Integrity is the quality of being able to be trusted. It means that we do not lie to one another, that we will do what we say we will do, that the affection we profess is genuine, and that the praise we give is honest.

To teach children to grow up like that can be difficult because honesty and integrity sometimes seem to be in short supply. "I'm so ashamed," a man said. "My teenage son has been helping a friend fix up a secondhand car, and the other day he told us how he had helped sell it, too. Know what he said? He said, 'Hey, Dad, I showed Brian that neat mileage trick you used when you got rid of the old Chevy.'" You see, we teach our children honesty—or dishonesty—by the way we ourselves live.

A little six-year-old boy was in a drugstore. He saw a comic book that he really wanted, but he had only a nickel. So when the storekeeper was not looking, the boy took the book. His parents found out and discussed what to do. They agreed that it had to be paid for, but could they not just take the money to the store and explain? After all, he's just a very little boy, and if they talked to him about it, they were certain he would never do it again. But no, they could not settle for that. They could not treat it that lightly. And a six-year-old boy accompanied by his parents went back to the store and told the owner what he had done, paid for the book, and asked for forgiveness.

Those parents were right! Honesty and integrity do not come without a price, and that lesson is best taught when children are young.

First of all, there is honesty.

Second, There Is Love

Remember what the apostle Paul said about love. He called it the "greatest of all," and "the best way of all." We need to give our children love, and lots of it. And we need to show them how to be loving persons, how to make *love* the theme of their lives and their stance toward the world.

In the book *The Miracle of Love* ([Old Tappan, N.J.: Fleming H. Revell Co., 1972], 75-76), Dr. Charles L. Allen tells about a man who consulted a noted psychiatrist about the best things he could do for his children. He made a list with categories for the best material things, the best education, good religious training, travel, culture, and social etiquette.

The psychiatrist said, "All these are extremely important, but you have not named the most important thing you can do for your children." The man wondered what he had not named. The psychiatrist replied, "The best thing you can do for your children is love their mother."

The best way to teach children how to be loving persons is to model love, to exemplify love, to live love in front of them, and to teach love, not only in words but also in our actions. Honesty and love: what wonderful gifts to give our children. But there is one other to be added, the one that holds them all together and makes honesty and love possible.

Third, of Course, Is Faith

Faith is not a small room stuck on the back of the house. It is the light in all the rooms. Faith enables us to be honest and loving. It's the golden thread that ties it all together. It is the cement that gives strength and endurance against the storms of life. It's the solid foundation, the undergirding, the strong rock.

Parents and grandparents, please tune in closely now: If you want to teach your children faith, the best way to do that is to let them see and experience your faith. Of course, teach them memorized prayers, but remember it's more important for them to see and hear you pray. Of course, encourage them to attend church and Sunday school, but remember that it's even more important for them to see you excited to be there.

Dr. Dick Murray was one of the leading Christian educators in America. He taught at Perkins School of Theology at Southern Methodist University. He was here some years ago to speak to our teachers, and he told about his four-year-old grandson, Martin. He said that he had taught Martin "Old MacDonald" and "Row, Row, Row Your Boat" and had decided that he needed to teach little Martin the Gloria Patri. So they got in the car, buckled up, and rode through the streets of Dallas, singing:

Glory be to the Father
And to the Son and to the Holy Ghost;
As it was in the beginning, is now, and ever shall be,
World without end. Amen. Amen.

("Glory Be to the Father," *The United Methodist Hymnal* [Nashville: United Methodist Publishing House, 1995], 70)

At the top of their lungs, granddaddy Dick Murray and four-year-old grandson Martin sang the Gloria Patri over and over and over, and they had a marvelous time. A short time later, Martin got to attend "big church" for the first time, and when they got to that place in the service where the congregation stood together and began to boldly sing the Gloria Patri, Dick Murray said he felt a tug on his coat. Martin was doing the tugging and was motioning for his granddad to bend down so he could tell him something. Dick Murray bent down, and four-year-old Martin said excitedly in his ear, "Poppa! Poppa! They are singing our song! They are singing our song!"

At the end of the day, will you be remembered as one who had a good and positive Christian influence on other people, and especially on children?

7

Will You Be Remembered . . .

As One Who Knew the Importance of Prayer?

Scripture: Luke 11:1-4

Let me begin with one of my favorite stories. It's called the legend of the touchstone. It is not a true story, but it is a great "truth story," one that serves as a haunting parable for you and me.

According to the legend, if you could find the touchstone on the coast of the Black Sea and hold it in your hand, everything you touched would turn to gold. You could recognize the touchstone by its warmth. All the other stones would feel cold, but the touchstone, as you picked it up, would turn warm in your hand.

Once, a man sold everything he had and went to the Black Sea in search of the touchstone. He began picking up every stone he could find on the coastline, wanting desperately to find the touchstone. After some days passed, he realized he was picking up the same stones again and again. So, he devised a plan: Pick up a stone; if it's cold, throw it into the sea. This he did for weeks and weeks. But then one morning, he came out early to continue his search for the touchstone. He picked up a stone. It was cold, and he threw it into the sea. He picked up another, and it was cold. He threw it into the sea. He picked up another and another and another. They were all cold, and he threw each into the sea.

He then picked up yet another stone. It turned warm in his hand, but before he realized what he was doing, he threw it into the sea! He had it in his hand, and he threw it away. So dulled by the routine, he did not recognize that stone's specialness, and, absentmindedly tossed it aside.

This can happen to us with the Lord's Prayer. We pick it up so often; we hear it so often. We repeat the words so often that if we are not careful, we miss the specialness, the power, the sacredness of the prayer. And before we realize what we are doing, we throw it away, toss it aside, fling it into the sea; and that is so sad.

What a treasure the Lord's Prayer is! And we have it in our hands. Jesus gave it to us. Please don't treat it casually or carelessly. Please don't routinely toss it aside. It is a sacred gift from our Lord. Remember how it's recorded in the Bible. The disciples of Jesus came to him one day and said, "Lord, teach us. Teach us to pray."

Notice something here. When did the disciples ask for this? When did they make this request? Was it after Jesus gave a lecture on prayer? No. Was it after Jesus led a seminar on prayer? No. Was it after Jesus preached a powerful sermon on prayer? No. None of these. Remember how Luke 11 describes it. Jesus was praying in a certain place, and when he finished, one of the disciples said to him, "Lord, teach us to pray." The point is clear: They saw what prayer meant to him and what it did for him. They saw the amazing spiritual power released in him by prayer, and they wanted that too. So in response to their request, Jesus taught them the Lord's Prayer, and as he did that, he gave them—and us—the key elements that lead to a meaningful prayer life.

There is so much to learn from the Lord's Prayer, so many directions to take. For example, the Lord's Prayer teaches us that Jesus himself prayed—regularly and sensibly and trustingly—and so can we. Or, another approach would be to examine how this great prayer underscores the "ACTS" of prayer, with the word *ACTS* serving as an acronym to remind us of the basic elements of prayer. The *A* stands for Adoration, the *C* stands for Confession, the *T* stands for Thanksgiving, and the *S* stands for Supplication (praying to God on behalf of others).

Still another way to come at this would be to underscore how the Lord's Prayer in its majesty and grandeur affirms the Trinity. The opening words celebrate God as the Father / Creator: "Our Father, who art in heaven, hallowed be thy name. Thy kingdom come, thy will be done on earth as it is in heaven. Give us this day our daily bread."

The middle words celebrate God as the Son and Savior: "Forgive us our trespasses, as we forgive those who trespass against us."

And later words celebrate God as the Holy Spirit, a Living Presence with us to guide, protect, comfort, and inspire: "Lead us not into temptation, but deliver us from evil."

All these approaches are interesting, but what I want to do in this chapter is simply ask this question: As Jesus gives his disciples the Lord's Prayer, what does he teach them and us about prayer? Jesus taught us many things, of course. But for now let me lift up three lessons that have been supremely helpful to me in my prayer life. Are you ready? Here is number one.

First of All, Jesus Teaches Us to Pray in the Spirit of Gratitude

If you spend time with Jesus, you will quickly and dramatically sense his incredible spirit of appreciation. If you draw close to him, you cannot miss his amazing spirit of thanksgiving and gratitude.

If someone called today and told us that we had just won a Mercedes-Benz automobile or a trip to Hawaii or twenty million dollars, we would probably be excited and grateful. But please notice that it is Jesus' enthusiasm for the little things—the seemingly ordinary and commonplace things—that really reveals his appreciative spirit.

Remember his frequent references to simple things like brooms, candles, leaven, old cloth, flowers, birds, mustard seeds, rocks, sunsets, the wind, the sky, the grass of the field, the faces of little children, and in the Lord's Prayer, our daily bread. These are the kinds of commonplace things that we too often take for granted. But all of these simple things spoke to Jesus and touched his heart and reminded him of the love and care of the Creator. He saw them as good and sacred gifts from the generous hand of our Father.

When you really stop to think about it, you realize that there is no such thing as an "ungrateful Christian." A

Christian by definition is one who accepts Christ and lives in the Spirit of Christ. And that means to live daily in the spirit of gratitude.

Max Lucado has a funny way of describing himself in his book *In the Grip of Grace* (Dallas : Word Publishing, 1996). He writes:

> Most of my life I've been a . . . closet slob. . . . Why make up a bed if you are going to sleep in it again tonight? . . . Isn't it easier to leave your clothes on the floor . . . so they'll be there when you get up . . . ?
>
> Then, I got married.
>
> Denalyn was so patient. She said she didn't mind my habits . . . if I didn't mind sleeping outside. . . .
>
> I enrolled in a twelve-step program for slobs. ("My name is Max, I hate to vacuum.") A physical therapist helped me rediscover the muscles used for hanging shirts and placing toilet paper on the holder. My nose was reintroduced to the fragrance of Pine Sol. . . .
>
> But then came the moment of truth. Denalyn went out of town for a week. . . . I figured I'd be a slob for six days and clean on the seventh. But . . . I couldn't relax with dirty dishes in the sink. . . .
>
> I'd been exposed to a "higher standard." (Pp. 116-17)

That's what happens to us when we really come into the presence of Christ. It changes us because we have been exposed to a higher standard. Our sloppy ways of selfishly grumbling and griping and complaining just don't feel right anymore because we have been exposed to his great spirit, to his high standard of appreciation and thanksgiving and gratitude.

Now, listen closely. I want to give you the greatest definition of prayer I have ever heard. It is so simple and yet so profound. Here it is: *Prayer is friendship with God.* If you will remember that, it will change your life, and it will change the way you pray. If prayer is, simply put, friendship with God, then that means we can talk to God the same way we talk to our best friend. We can lay out our fears, our concerns, our worries, our successes, our disappointments, our problems, our joys, our sorrows, and our dreams and know that God will understand and will love us and help us and support us come what may, because he is our Best Friend. But I also believe that whatever we bring to God, we should bring it in the spirit of gratitude. In the Lord's Prayer, Jesus teaches us that we should pray in the spirit of gratitude.

Second, Jesus Teaches Us to Pray in the Spirit of Forgiveness

Right in the middle of the Lord's Prayer we find these words: "Forgive us our trespasses, as we forgive those who trespass against us." Jesus is teaching us again the crucial lesson about forgiveness that he taught so often and that we need so desperately to hear and understand, namely, that we need to be forgiven and we need to be forgivers.

We accept God's forgiveness, and then we pass that forgiveness on to others. We receive forgiveness from our Lord, and then we become "echoes" of his forgiving spirit in the world. Or, put another way, we cannot come fully into the presence of God with hatred and hostility in our hearts.

Remember how Jesus put this so dramatically in the Sermon on the Mount. He said that if you come to the altar and remember that someone has something against you, go fix that, go reconcile that, and then come back to the altar. But you may say, "Now, wait a minute; it's not *my* fault!" Of course it's not your fault, but as a Christian it is your responsibility to fix it because the spiritual poisons of hatred, hostility, resentment, and bitterness will contaminate your spirit and devastate your soul.

Let me show you what I mean. One of Leonardo da Vinci's most famous creations is his painting of the Lord's Supper. It is said that while Da Vinci was working on the painting, he got into an argument with a fellow painter. Da Vinci was so mad at this colleague that, in anger and out of spite, he used that man's face as the face of Judas in his painting.

But then, having completed Judas's face, Da Vinci turned to paint the face of Christ, and he could not do it. It would not come; he could not visualize it. He could not paint the face of Christ. He put down his paintbrush, and he went to find his enemy and to forgive him. They both apologized, and they both forgave. That very evening Da Vinci had a dream, and in that dream he saw the face of Christ. He rose quickly from his bed and finished the painting, and it became one of his greatest masterpieces.

The point is this: Leonardo da Vinci could not portray the face of Christ with hostility in his heart. And neither can we! We come to God for our forgiveness. Then we are called to live in God's generous, gracious, forgiving Spirit. Someone expressed it like this:

> You cannot pray the Lord's Prayer
> And even once say "I";

> You cannot pray the Lord's Prayer
> And even once say "My."
>
> Nor can you pray the Lord's Prayer
> And not pray for one another;
> And when you ask for daily bread,
> You must include your brother.
>
> For others are included
> In each and every plea;
> From the beginning to the end of it,
> It does not once say "Me."

In the Lord's Prayer, Jesus teaches us to pray in the spirit of gratitude and in the spirit of forgiveness.

Third and Finally, Jesus Teaches Us to Pray in the Spirit of Trust

Some years ago when I was in seminary, I had a classmate from Michigan named Paul. He had an amazing experience back in the 1950s as a U.S. soldier in Korea. One night while out on a scouting patrol, Paul zigged when he should have zagged, and he got lost. Inadvertently, he wandered above the 38th Parallel into enemy territory. For several days, he hid out in the wilderness, but eventually he was captured and was made a prisoner of war. It was a horrible experience beyond words.

On two occasions, Paul was compelled by the enemy to dig his own grave and then stand in front of it as a firing squad marched out, raised their rifles, aimed at him, and on command, squeezed their triggers. But nothing happened. The rifles did not fire, the hammers fell shut on empty guns. It was a form of torture.

One day, in the midst of the cold North Korean winter, his captors poured ice water on Paul's head, over and over again, bucket after bucket, until he became the victim of complete amnesia. He could not remember anything. In fact, the only thing Paul could remember was that he could not remember! It was a "dark night of the soul" for Paul. He didn't know who he was, where he was, where he had come from, or what he was doing there. He didn't even know his own name!

Day after day, night after night, hour after hour, he sat in that prison camp, trying desperately to remember something, trying frantically to pull something out of his suddenly darkened past. Finally, after a long struggle, he remembered something—two words: "Our Father." Just those two words. He didn't know what they meant or where they had come from, but he knew they represented something from the past. So he began to repeat those two words, "Our Father . . . Our Father . . . Our Father," hoping that something else would come back to him out of his lost memory.

Well, something else did come: "Our Father, *who art in heaven.*" Then he repeated that phrase over and over until he remembered "hallowed be thy name." He went on like that until he had reconstructed the entire Lord's Prayer, and then he remembered his parents, who had taught him the prayer. Then he remembered his church, his neighborhood, his friends, his country, his mission there, and finally, he remembered his name!

Isn't that something? Paul rebuilt his life and his memory around the Lord's Prayer, and uniquely around those two opening words, "Our Father." Paul not only survived that experience, but also ironically came out of it with two things he had never had before—a call to the ministry and, amazingly, a photographic memory!

Now, I don't want any of us to have to go through what Paul went through, but wouldn't it be something if every one of us could rediscover ourselves and rebuild our lives around the Lord's Prayer, and especially around those two words, "Our Father"? If we could really know God as a loving, caring parent who knows what is best for us, then every prayer and every day would be entrusted to him and to the doing of his will. As one of my older, saintly friends put it in her prayers, "Lord, here's what *I* would like, but have it *your* way, 'cause you're a lot smarter than *I* am."

In the Lord's Prayer, Jesus teaches us to pray in the spirit of gratitude, in the spirit of forgiveness, and in the spirit of trust.

8

Will You Be Remembered . . .

As One Who Knew
Right from Wrong?

Scripture: Matthew 7:13-20; Romans 7:15

Have you ever wondered what goes through the minds of children and young people these days as they watch the six o'clock news? What are they learning? What are they thinking? How does it influence them to hear stories like those broadcast on one Friday night a few years ago, stories about

- a professional athlete attacking his coach and threatening his life;
- a schoolteacher being sent to prison for having an affair with a thirteen-year-old student;
- a man posing as a banker and bilking a Roman Catholic priest out of fourteen million dollars of the church's money;
- a movie director beating up his famous movie star girlfriend and then saying it was just a misunderstanding between two good friends;
- a newborn baby abandoned by her mother in a restroom at Disney World;

- a Houston police officer fighting for her life after being shot in a drug bust;
- threats of war and sordid allegations flying fast and furious in our nation's capital.

One question that emerges out of all this is, How do we equip our children and our young people (and indeed, ourselves) to know when something is wrong? Right? Wrong? Good? Bad? Ethical? Unethical? How can we tell the difference? What are some specific guidelines for a perplexed conscience? What are some helpful, concrete, practical tests for making moral decisions? Let's face it. It is not always easy these days to tell the difference between right and wrong. People in today's society do get confused, mixed up, led astray, in making ethical decisions; so, the question is, are our decisions right? wrong? good? bad? moral? immoral? And how do we tell the difference?

Most of us can identify with the little boy who brought home a report card with terrible grades in conduct. His only explanation was, "But, Mom, conduct is my hardest subject!" That's true for most of us. Again and again we find it hard to do right. Conduct is indeed our hardest subject.

Remember how poignantly Paul expressed this in his letter to the Romans. The J. B. Phillips translation puts it graphically: "My own behaviour baffles me. For I find myself doing what I really loathe but not doing what I really want to do. . . . I often find that I have the will to do good, but not the power. . . . It is an agonizing situation" (7:15-24 JBP). This is one passage of Scripture that needs no explanation. We know what Paul means here. How well we know from our own experience!

Several weeks ago, one of our church's college students who attends school in another state came home for a few days and stopped by to see me. We chatted for a while about family, friends, and the church. Her face suddenly grew serious, and she blurted out: "Jim, I'm so confused! Life on the college campus is hard. Sometimes it is so difficult to tell right from wrong. I don't want to compromise my standards. I don't want to let go of my Christian beliefs and values, but I don't want to be a prude or a religious snob either. The pressure is so terrific sometimes, so unrelenting. It's easy to get confused, to rationalize, to give in. Can you help me? Can you give me some practical, down-to-earth guidelines for making moral decisions?"

I said to her, "Let's work at it together." So we took out a pad and a pencil and began to brainstorm about this. We made a practical list of tests for right and wrong. Right? Wrong? How do we tell the difference? This is what we put on our list. Let me invite you to try these on for size.

First, There Is the Test of Plain Common Sense

It is a fact of history that common sense has shown us that some things, which were at one time considered honorable and respectable, were in fact ridiculous.

Harry Emerson Fosdick was reported to have used the example of dueling. Many years ago, the practice of dueling was believed to be honorable. But today, if someone challenged you to a duel, you would say, "Don't be ridiculous! Don't be silly!"

Common sense did not just argue dueling out of existence, it laughed it out of existence. Common sense rose up and said, "Don't be ridiculous! Don't be silly!"

Don't you wonder about what things we are doing today that will be called silly and ridiculous by history? If we could get into a time machine and go one hundred or two hundred or five hundred years into the future and look back, what do you think would be the things we are doing these days that will have been laughed out of existence, eliminated by plain common sense?

Listen! If you are tempted to fight or to drink excessively or to play around with sex, if you are tempted to smoke or cheat or lie or steal or gossip or hate or dabble with dangerous mind-bending drugs, then let your common sense rise up and say to your soul: "Don't be silly!" A good, healthy dose of what the old-timers used to call "horse sense" would serve us all well, even in our moral dilemmas.

Recently, while on a speaking engagement in another city, I went into a restaurant late one night. This particular restaurant was located near a college campus, and a lot of students were there. It was about 10:30 at night. Some of the college guys, perhaps feeling restless from the pressures of school, needed to let off steam. Someone in the group shouted out that they should go start a fight with the Baptist College across town. Quickly, it became a mob scene, with a lot of wild-eyed cheering and sneering. Everybody was churned up, feeling macho and ready to fight. Everybody, that is, except a mature upperclassman named Joe, who was sitting quietly in the corner, thumbing through one of his textbooks.

Then this exchange took place: "Aren't you going with us, Joe?" someone shouted. Quietly, Joe looked up from his book. Silence overtook the room. All eyes were on Joe. "No, I'm not going," Joe said in a steady voice. "What's the matter? You scared?" came the retort. Joe closed his book and placed it on the table before him. He looked at the mob and said, "No, it's not that I'm scared. I'm not going because it's dumb! It's dumb, stupid, adolescent, dangerous, and destructive. When people fight, nobody wins! It's childish and ridiculous!"

Suddenly, the mob scene was over. Now, they may have fought later, but for the moment, Joe's common sense had won the day. He had jolted their consciences, stopped the stampede, brought them back to their senses. This is a good test for moral decisions, isn't it? Does this thing I'm contemplating make sense or is it silly, adolescent, and ridiculous?

Second, There Is the Test of Publicity

What if it were brought out in the open? What if everybody knew what you were proposing to do? Would you still do it?

This moral decision, this perplexing thing, this conduct we are not quite sure of: Put it to the test of publicity. Strip it of its secrecy. Get it out in the light. Bring it out in the open air. Imagine it written up in the morning newspaper or broadcast on the six o'clock television news. Do you want your parents to know about it? Or your children? And what about your friends? Would you want them to know? Imagine it talked about openly. Imagine it written in the story of your life for your children and grand-children to read. This is one of the healthiest tests for morality there is.

Phillips Brooks put it dramatically. He said, "To keep clear of concealment, to keep clear of the need [for] concealment . . . do nothing which [you] might not do out on the middle of Boston Common at noon-day. . . . It is an awful hour when the first necessity of hiding anything comes. The whole life is different thenceforth when there are questions to be feared and eyes to be avoided . . . the bloom of life is gone. Put off that day as long as possible. Put it off forever if you can" (Harry Emerson Fosdick, *Twelve Tests of Character* [New York: Richard R. Smith, 1931], 46).

Precisely so! You see, things that cannot stand the light are not healthy! So, this is a pretty good test. If what you are doing or thinking about doing can stand the test of publicity, then it's probably all right. If not, it is suspect! It's probably wrong!

Third, There Is the Test of Your Best Self

If we are going to become mature Christians, then somewhere along the way, we have to grow up. We have to step out on our own and stand on our own two feet. We have to stop following the crowd and decide who we want to be, and then we must be true to that best self. This, too, is a pretty good test for morality. "Can I do this thing and still be true to my best self?"

Recently, a good friend came by to see me. He told me about a recent business opportunity that would have made him a wealthy man. But he turned it down because it had some shady angles. "I couldn't do it," he said. "I just couldn't do it and live with myself."

Ralph Sockman once reminded us of that old prayer of confession out of the ancient church that said, "O Lord, we have erred and strayed from thy ways like lost sheep." Sockman went on to say that the greatest temptation of Christians today is to become herd-minded—always to nibble around at the ground, automatically to follow the herd, and never to look up and find our own direction, our own identity, our own standards, our own morality, our own best self.

If you have a perplexed conscience, if you are facing an ethical dilemma or a moral decision, if you are trying to distinguish between right and wrong, then try the test of the best self. "Can I participate in this? Can I do this thing and still be true to my best self?" There is the test of common sense, the test of publicity, and the test of your best self.

And Finally, There Is the Test of Christ

This is where Paul found himself. "Wretched man that I am!" he said. "Who will rescue me from this body of death? Thanks be to God through Jesus Christ our Lord!" (Romans 7:24-25). If you feel confused or perplexed or bewildered, and you wonder what is right and what is wrong, then bring your thoughts back home to Christi-anity's one unique truth: Jesus of Nazareth! He is our pattern, our blueprint, our measuring stick, our Savior! Matthew 7 tells us that a sound tree cannot produce evil fruit. Well, the way we stay sound is to stay close to Jesus Christ.

Here are the key questions to ask: "Can I do this and still be in the Spirit of Christ? Can I say this and still be in the Spirit of Christ? Can I participate in this and still be in the Spirit of Christ?" If not, don't do it, because it's *wrong*. The poet John Greenleaf Whittier put it like this:

> O Lord and Master of us all!
> Whate'er our name or sign,
> We own Thy sway, we hear Thy call,
> We test our lives by Thine.
>
> . . . .
>
> We faintly hear, we dimly see,
> In differing phrase we pray;
> But, dim or clear, we own in Thee
> The Light, the Truth, the Way!

("Our Master," 1866)

How do we tell when something is right or wrong? We test it. We apply the test of common sense, the test of publicity, the test of our best self. But most important, we apply the test of Christ!

9

Will You Be Remembered . . .

As One Who Knew the Significance of the Battle Within?

Scripture: Acts 9:1-9

Let me begin this chapter with a couple of quick stories. See if you can find the common thread that runs through them and links them together.

Story number one comes from Joe Garagiola. Joe Garagiola, as many of you will remember, is a former major-league baseball player and a former cohost of NBC's *The Today Show*. He tells about an experience he had when he went shopping in a drugstore one morning. He said he selected a bottle of extra strength Tylenol, a twelve-ounce bottle of Kaopectate, an elastic knee brace, a back support, a supply of corn plasters, some Dristan, a remedy for sore gums, and a large tube of Ben Gay. He took all that stuff to the counter, and the clerk rang it up on the register. Then as she handed Joe his purchases, she said "Have a nice day!"

The second story is about a woman who gave birth to her child in a hospital elevator while on her way to the maternity ward. She was highly embarrassed by all the trouble and commotion she had caused. She apologized profusely to those taking care of her. "That's all right, Ma'am," said one attendant. "This is nothing. Last year, I delivered a baby out there on the front lawn. The woman never even made it into the hospital." "I know," said the exasperated woman, "that was me, too!"

Now, of course, the common thread that runs through these stories is the dramatic reminder that life can be hard, life can be tough, life can be a battle. But the truth is that as hard as the battles are out there in our rough-and-tumble world, the real crucial battles are those that take place inside of us. The battle within: *That's* where the rubber meets the road. The battle within: That's where the most significant victories are won or lost. The battle within: That's where we choose the way of light or the way of darkness.

Mark Trotter talked about this in a sermon, using a powerful illustration. In 1952, a writer named Bernard Malamud wrote a classic novel on this theme. The story was called *The Natural* (New York: Harcourt Brace). Many of you probably saw the film version of this book. Robert Redford played the title role of baseball player Roy Hobbs. It's a great book and a great movie. Roy Hobbs is "the natural." The name itself implies innocence. Natural means unspoiled, untainted. It's the way things are supposed to be. Roy Hobbs is like that. He is like Adam in the Garden of Eden. He is like all of us before temptation. He has a life of great promise. He is a natural athlete, a natural baseball player.

He is born on a farm in Nebraska, and his father realizes quickly that Roy has enormous baseball talent. Roy's father cultivates that talent. His dad works with him and teaches him how to play. But one day, his father dies. Coincidentally, on that very day, a lightning bolt strikes a tree on the farm. Roy Hobbs takes a piece of wood from that tree, shapes it into a bat, and takes the bat with him on the rest of his journey—into the major leagues of baseball.

Immediately, young Roy Hobbs is tempted by the corruption of the game, by agents and hangers-on who try to trick him, and especially by a woman who in the book and movie is the classic image of temptation. When Roy rejects her, she takes a gun and shoots him. Wounded physically and emotionally, Roy Hobbs runs away, retreats, leaves the game, and goes into obscurity, saying, "My life didn't turn out the way I expected."

But at the age of thirty-five, he makes a comeback. He returns to the major leagues. Once again, temptation confronts him, this time in the form of the owner of the team, who is the personification of evil. He's a man who cannot stand light. He is allergic to light, so he has to be in darkness all the time. He has his office in a skybox, high above the stadium. He sits in the darkness and looks out over all that he owns, including Roy Hobbs.

The story comes to a climax during a game. The evil owner is sitting in the darkness, and the temptress has now joined him, because it is revealed that she works for him. They want Roy Hobbs to throw the game. They have a huge bet on the game, and they tempt and threaten Roy and demand that he do what they say. But there is another woman who enters the story, one who symbolizes redemption. She is in the stands behind the home-team dugout. She is wearing white, and she is surrounded by light. She sends a message to Roy Hobbs, a message that strengthens him and emboldens him and gives him the courage to do the right thing.

I will not tell you precisely how the story ends, but I will tell you this: It is spectacular! It's one of the great victory moments in all of motion picture history. The point is this. In that scene, the writer Bernard Malamud paints the human condition: Roy Hobbs at the plate, having to make a decision about his life, doing battle within. In what direction will he go? Will he choose good or evil, right or wrong, light or darkness? Temptation on one side of him, pulling him, pushing him, enticing him, threatening him in one direction, and on the other an angel of light who is for him and who wants to help him.

Mark Trotter puts it like this: "This is what life is all about. It's as old as Adam and Eve. It says that there are forces inside of you and outside of you that will lead you into lives that you will regret, lives of pain and guilt and sorrow and darkness. So don't be naive about this. Don't assume that just because you are intelligent or well educated that reason is going to lead you safely through this life. Don't be naive. Reason can be bought or seduced, just as easily, indeed maybe even more easily, than any other human faculty. That is why Jesus instructed us to pray daily, 'Lead us not into temptation,' because we will need grace, we will need strength from beyond ourselves, to lead a meaningful, fulfilled and moral life."

This "battle within," between light and darkness, is played out powerfully for us in the Scripture lesson in Acts 9. Here we see Saul of Tarsus doing battle within, grappling with his soul. Look at how it starts with the words of darkness: "Meanwhile Saul, still breathing threats and murder against the disciples of the Lord, went to the high priest and asked him for letters to the synagogues at Damascus, so that if he found any who belonged to the Way, men or women, he might bring them bound to Jerusalem" (vv. 1-2). Saul, like an ecclesiastical bounty hunter, heads toward Damascus in the spirit of darkness, in the spirit of self-righteousness and arrogance and prejudice and resentment and greed and hostility, breathing (as the Bible puts it) threats and murder.

But then comes the light, a light from heaven. It flashes about him, scares him out of his wits, and Saul falls to the ground in fear. "Saul, Saul," a voice calls out to him from the light, "why do you persecute me?" (v. 4). In other words, "Why are you choosing the way of darkness?" Saul stammers out a question, "Who are you, Lord?" The answer comes out of the light: "I am Jesus, whom you are persecuting." Saul was scared to death before, and now he is really shaking in his boots. He knows he is about to get it in the neck. He waits for the ax to fall.

But instead of punishing Saul, Jesus says, in essence, "Saul, I want you on my team. Don't fight against us anymore. I know about all the terrible things you've done to hurt my cause. But I forgive you and want you on my side. Come out of the darkness and into the light. Come join my team." In that moment, Saul was bowled over by amazing grace, and he walked out of the darkness and into the light. And from that moment forward, everything he said or did or wrote went back to that day when he grappled with his soul on the road to Damascus, and he remembered how Christ gave him love and forgiveness and the strength to win the battle. We know this story personally, don't we? Every day, in a spiritual sense, we walk the Damascus road. Every day, we grapple with our souls. Every day, we fight temptation. Every day, we do battle within. Let me show you what I mean with three thoughts.

First of All, Every Day We Do Battle Within Regarding How We Relate to This World

Is life in this world a blessing or a curse? Is life in this world a joy or a grind? Is it a problem or an opportunity? Is it a gift or a prison? An endurance test or a celebration? With regard to this world and our life within it, that is the battle that rages within us each and every day—indeed, each and every moment. Will we embrace life or will we resent life?

Ron DelBene, in his book *From the Heart* (Nashville: Upper Room Books, 1991), shares an experience of a few years ago. It had been an especially hectic week, and on this particular morning, he had to get up at 5:00 A.M. to make it to a 6:30 A.M. class he was teaching at his church. As he pulled into the parking lot at the church, he saw a woman cutting across the church parking lot. He guessed that since it was so early (and given the direction she was headed), she was a maid on her way to work. It was a brisk morning, and she was bundled up to protect herself from the cold.

As she passed Ron, he stifled a yawn and said, "Another day, another dollar." She broke stride momentarily, and with a bright and warm smile that lit up her face, she responded to him with a lilt in her voice, "Yes, and ain't it a blessing! Ain't it a blessing!" Ron watched her as she went on her way, but he was jolted and moved by her response. He imagined that she had probably gotten up an hour before he did, had ridden a bus downtown, and transferred to a second bus to reach this neighborhood so early. She would probably spend her day looking after someone's children or cleaning another family's house. And yet, she saw the day as a blessing, while Ron had let himself see it as a grind. But she had jolted him back to reality and to the blessing of the day and of life. He looked around and began to drink in the beauty of the early morning, and he said to himself, *This is the day the Lord has made; I will rejoice and be glad in it!*

What would it do for us if we saw every day as a blessing instead of a grind? What would it do for us if we began every day by saying, "Good morning, Lord!" instead of "Good Lord, it's morning!"? What would it do for us if we began each day saying, "This is the day the Lord has made; I will rejoice and be glad in it!"

That's number one. Every single day of our lives, we do battle within regarding how we relate to this world.

Second, Every Day We Do Battle Within Regarding How We Relate to Other People

The musical *Godspell* has many wonderful scenes. One of my favorites is a scene toward the end when Jesus is with his disciples in the Upper Room. He takes a bucket of water, a rag, and a mirror, and he goes to his disciples, each in turn, and washes away their painted clown faces. Then he holds the mirror up in front of them, so they can see themselves as they really are. And then, he hugs them!

The point is clear and powerful: We don't have to wear false faces, we don't have to hide our inadequacies, we don't have to pretend. God loves us and accepts us, just as we are!

That's what Paul discovered on the road to Damascus when the risen Lord spoke to him: "Paul, I know about you. I know what you've been up to, but I still love you. I still accept you, and I still want you on my side!" And that is exactly what Jesus says to you and me: "I know all about you. I know all about your sins, your failures, your weaknesses, your shortcomings. I know all about your inadequacies, but I still love you, I still accept you, and I want you on my team."

This is the Christian faith in three words: *We are accepted.* God loves us. God loves and accepts us graciously. Now, here's the other side of that coin: God wants us to accept that love and pass it on to other people. He wants us to live in that same kind of gracious, loving spirit. He wants us to imitate his generosity in our dealings with others. He wants us to extend to other people the same kind of "amazing grace" that he has extended to us. That's the measuring stick of Christian love—to be as generous and gracious and forgiving toward others as God in Christ has been generous and gracious and forgiving toward us.

Let me share something with you that I think is terrific. It's a piece written by Diane Loomans called "If I Had My Child to Raise Over Again" (Diane Loomans and Julia Loomans, *Full Esteem Ahead* [Tiburon, Calif.: H J Kramer, 1994], 194). Loomans says that if she were to raise her child again, her priorities and decisions about her child would be different. For example, she says she would "finger paint more, and point the finger less" and "do less correcting, and more connecting." Even small actions such as running through fields and gazing at stars more often would have changed the way she parented her child. She ends the poem hoping that she has been a model of the power of love rather than the love of power.

Isn't that great? You know what the parent who wrote that was saying? Simply this: If I had it all to do over again, I would see my child not as a problem to be solved, but as a gift to be celebrated. And you know, when you stop to think about it, that is precisely the way to relate to every person we meet and that is the Christian calling—to see the other person not as a problem to be solved, not as a thing to be used, not as a nuisance to be endured, not as an adversary to be defeated, but as a gift to be celebrated. Every day, we do battle within regarding how we relate to life ("Is life for me a joy or a grind?") and how we relate to other people ("Are they problems or gifts?").

Third and Finally, Every Day We Do Battle Within Regarding How We Relate to God and the Church

All of us who are members of the church stood at the altar and made a sacred promise to God. We promised to be loyal to the church and to support it with our prayers, our presence, our gifts, and our service. We stood at the altar and made that promise to God, and yet the real truth is that too many of us (far too many of us) are more realistically described by the hymn parody "I'll Go Where You Want Me to Go, Dear Lord."

Essentially, the parody underscores one of our main challenges as christian people—the difficulty of unwavering commitment to the Lord. The parody shows how we often claim that we want to do whatever God calls us to do, but then quickly we begin to qualify or water down our response: "Here I am, Lord. Use me as you will, but just don't ask me to sing in the church choir. Here I am, Lord, your humble and willing servant, but just don't expect me to teach Sunday school . . . or tithe." The parody then closes with these haunting words: "I'm busy just now with myself, dear Lord; I'll help you some other day."

Does any of that sound at all familiar? It's the battle within: "Will we be loyal to God and the church or not?"

Let me ask you something: How is it with you right now? How's the battle going? Are you really committed to celebrating life in the world? Are you really committed to loving other people? Are you really committed to serving God and the church? At the end of the day, will you be remembered as one who knew the significance of the battle within, and as one who dealt with it creatively and redemptively?

─ぐ**10**ぐ─

Will You Be Remembered . . .

As One Who Knew
the Power of Words?

Scripture: Luke 7:1-10

Sister Helen Mrosia is a teacher at Saint Mary's School in Minnesota. She tells a touching story about an experience she had with some of her students some years ago. Sister Helen was teaching third-graders that year, and she loved all of her students. But one third-grader named Mark Eklund was one in a million. Mark was always neat in appearance but also had a carefree attitude that made even his mischievousness delightful.

Mark talked incessantly during class, and Sister Helen had to remind him that talking without permission was not acceptable. But what impressed Sister Helen so much was Mark's sincere response every time he was corrected for misbehaving: "Thank you for correcting me, Sister." Sister Helen did not know what to make of that at first but became accustomed to hearing it many times a day.

One morning, Sister Helen's patience grew thin when Mark talked once too often. She looked at Mark and said, "If you say one more word, I am going to tape your mouth shut!" Ten seconds later, Chuck, a classmate, blurted out, "Sister, Mark is talking again!" Sister Helen had not asked the students to help her watch Mark, but she had stated the punishment in front of the class and had to act on it.

Sister Helen walked to her desk, opened the drawer, and took out a roll of masking tape. She walked to Mark's desk, tore off two pieces of tape, and made a big "X" over Mark's mouth. She returned to the front of the room and glanced at Mark. Then Mark winked at her. Sister Helen started laughing. The class cheered as she walked back to Mark's desk and removed the tape. Mark's first words were, "Thank you for correcting me, Sister."

At the end of the year, Sister Helen was asked to teach junior-high math. The years flew by, and Mark was in her classroom again. He was more handsome than ever and just as polite. Since he had to listen carefully to learn math, Mark did not talk as much in ninth grade as he had in third. One Friday, things just did not feel right. The class had worked hard on a new concept all week, and the students were frustrated with themselves and edgy with one another. Sister Helen felt that she needed to stop all this crankiness before it got out of hand, so she did an interesting thing. She asked them to list the names of the other students in the room on two sheets of paper and leave a space between each name. Then she told them to think of the nicest thing they could say about each of their classmates and write it down. This activity took the remainder of the class period.

To finish the assignment, as the students left the room, each one handed his or her paper to Sister Helen. One student named Charlie smiled, and Mark said, "Thank you for teaching me, Sister. Have a good weekend."

That Saturday, Sister Helen wrote down the name of each student on a separate sheet of paper, and then she listed what everyone else had said about that individual. On Monday, she gave each student his or her list, and the entire class was eventually smiling again. "I never knew that meant anything to anyone," someone said. "I didn't know others like me so much," somebody else said. No one ever mentioned those papers in class again, but it did not matter because the exercise was successful. The students were happy with themselves and with one another again.

Several years later, Sister Helen returned home from a vacation, and her parents met her plane. Riding home, Sister Helen sensed an uneasiness in the car. "Dad," she said, "is something wrong?" Her father cleared his throat as he always did before something important. "The Eklunds called last night," he began. "Really?" Sister Helen said. "I haven't heard from them in years. I wonder how Mark is." Her father responded quietly, "Mark was killed in Vietnam. The funeral is tomorrow, and his parents would like for you to come."

Sister Helen went to the funeral the next day. It seemed so unreal that Mark, who had been so young and so fine and so full of life, could be gone. As she looked at Mark in the casket, Sister Helen thought, *I'd give all the masking tape in the world if Mark would talk to me now.* After the funeral, most of Mark's former classmates headed to Chuck's farmhouse for lunch. Mark's mother and father were there, waiting for Sister Helen. "We want to show you something," Mark's father said. He pulled out a wallet. "This is Mark's wallet. They found it on Mark when he was killed. There's something in here, Sister Helen, that I think you will recognize."

Opening the billfold, he carefully removed two worn pieces of notebook paper that had been taped and folded and refolded many times. Sister Helen knew immediately what it was. It was the list of all the good things Mark's classmates had said about him way back in junior high. "Thank you so much for doing that," Mark's mother said. "As you can see, Mark treasured it."

Then an amazing thing happened. Mark's former classmates were watching this and suddenly began talking at once. Charlie blurted out, "I still have my list! It's in the top drawer of my desk at home." Marilyn said, "I have mine, too. It's in my diary." Chuck's wife said, "Chuck asked me to put his list in our wedding album, and I did." Then Vicki, another classmate, reached into her purse and took out her wallet and showed her worn and frazzled list to the group. "I carry my list with me at all times. I think we all saved our lists." Sister Helen sat down and cried. She cried for Mark and for those who would miss him, and she cried because she was so touched that they had all kept their lists.

Sister Helen said she learned a great lesson that day, a lesson about the power of words, a lesson about how the words of empathy and love and encouragement can so dramatically influence the life of another person. People are hungry for the words that lift and heal.

Now, that's what the Scripture lesson in Luke 7 is all about. A Roman centurion asked Jesus to heal his servant with words: "Just say the word and my servant will be healed." What a powerful verse that is. Remember the story with me.

As Jesus came into the city of Capernaum, the centurion made an unusual request through his Jewish friends. "Lord," he said, "my servant is gravely ill. I'm so worried about him. He is in terrible distress. He needs your help." Jesus was touched by the extraordinary compassion of this Roman centurion, because at that time, many masters were quite ruthless with their slaves. They often treated servants contemptibly, treating them like objects or living tools and using them up for all they were worth; and when they became unable to work or produce, the master would just discard them—casually, unfeelingly, and, sometimes, even brutally.

But this centurion was different. He loved this slave like a member of his family. He was deeply grieved over the slave's illness and was determined to do everything he could to help. Jesus was impressed by the centurion and said, "I will come and heal him." But the centurion answered, "Lord, I am not worthy to have you come under my roof; but just say the word, and my servant will be healed." Jesus was moved by his faith, and he replied, "Go; let it be done for you according to your faith" (Matthew 8:13; compare Matthew 8:5-13); and the servant was healed! End of story.

Now, at this point we could go in several different directions. We could examine the great faith of this Roman centurion, a faith so strong that it impressed Jesus. Or we could discuss the marvelous capacity of Jesus to bridge the gap between different nations, even between Jews and

Romans. Or we could look at the awesome power of Jesus to heal people, even from long distance. But for now, let me invite you to zero in on the healing power of words: "Just say the words, and healing will come."

Of course, we all know that Jesus could speak the words of healing, but on a lesser level, in a different dimension, yet in a significant way, so can we! This is the calling of the church—to continue the preaching, teaching, caring, healing ministry of Christ. And one way we can fulfill that calling is by speaking those powerful words that can bring healing to hurting hearts and wholeness to broken and grieving spirits. Let me show you what I mean.

First of All, We Can Speak the Words of Empathy

A few summers ago while on vacation, a minister friend of mine worshiped in another church. He said the associate pastor preached a splendid sermon, and it was a nice service. But something happened that morning that the congregation is still talking about. It occurred following the offering, when the ushers bring the offering back to the altar. Normally, the organist plays the Doxology, and the people stand and sing as the offering is presented. In this church, the organ is programmed so that one can simply push a button and the Doxology can be played without the organist present. However, someone had changed the stops on the organ the previous evening, and just as two burly male ushers walked down the aisle, side by side, with the offering plates, the organ played not the Doxology, but the wedding march.

As the congregation broke into laughter, and as the

organist scrambled to push the button that abruptly stopped the music, one of the ushers loudly exclaimed, "I do!" Just the right words for the moment. Don't you admire those special people who know how to come up with just the right words at the right time? This is especially true with the words of empathy. If "sympathy" means to feel sorry for somebody, then "empathy" means to feel sorry *with* somebody. It means to feel their hurt, to experience their pain, to walk in their shoes.

Last week, I conducted the funeral service for one of our saints. Her name was Esther, and she was a sweet, sweet spirit. Her daughter, Marcella, told me a wonderful story about Esther that captured her essence. Isn't it something, how sometimes one life vignette can encapsulate who a person is? Marcella said it happened on one Thanksgiving Day when Marcella was about five years old. Esther had worked hard for days on this Thanksgiving feast, using her special china and silver and an exquisite white-linen tablecloth. The food was ready, everything was perfect, and the family had gathered.

But five-year-old Marcella wanted to help her mother, so Esther let her put the water glasses on the table. Marcella completed that task and then ran to get a glass of chocolate milk for herself. Just as she was placing it on the table, the glass slipped out of her little fingers, and chocolate milk went all over the white tablecloth! Some parents, at that moment, would have gone ballistic, but Esther never blinked an eye. She said, "Oops! Marcella, we had an accident, didn't we? It's okay. We'll just clean it up." They cleaned it up the best they could, and Marcella ran to the kitchen to get another glass of chocolate milk. And, would you believe it, it slipped out of her hands again and smashed to the floor. Chocolate milk and pieces of glass went everywhere!

What would you have said in that moment if you were Esther? Let me tell you what Esther said. She said, "Marcella, there must be something wrong with that chocolate milk. I guess you just weren't supposed to drink it." Marcella grew up and became a very fine doctor in our city. And to this day, when you say, "Marcella, tell me about your mother; what was she like?" Marcella remembers vividly that Thanksgiving Day years ago, when her mother spoke the words of empathy. Just the perfect words a little five-year-old girl needed to hear in that moment.

Just say the words of empathy, and healing will come.

Second, We Can Speak the Words of Love

It has been documented time and again that love promotes healing. That's what the movie *Patch Adams* is about—when we see people hurting and we want to help them, the best thing we can do is to let them know we love them, to speak the words of love and call them by name.

Her name is Joanie. She was in her second month of nursing school when the professor gave a pop quiz. Joanie was a good student, and she breezed through all the questions until she came to the last one. The question was, "What is the first name of the woman who cleans the school?" Joanie thought, *Surely this is some kind of joke.* She had seen the cleaning lady every day. She was a tall woman with dark hair, probably in her fifties. But Joanie had no idea what her name was. Joanie turned in her test paper, leaving the last question blank.

Another student asked if the last question would count toward the quiz grade. "Absolutely," said the professor. "In your careers, you will meet many people. All of them are significant. All of them are important. All of them deserve your attention and love and care and kindness." Joanie said later, "I never forgot that lesson; I also learned that the cleaning lady's name was Dorothy."

Just say the words of empathy and love, and healing will come.

Third and Finally, We Can Speak the Words of Encouragement

In the book *Mistreated* ([Portland, Ore.: Multnomah, 1989], 3), Ron Lee Davis tells about two altar boys. One was born in 1892 in Eastern Europe. The other was born in 1895 in a small town in Illinois. The boys lived different lives in very different parts of the world but had an almost identical experience. When they were young, each boy assisted his parish priest in serving Mass. Ironically, each boy accidentally spilled wine on the carpet while handling the chalice. Each boy was embarrassed, ashamed, and afraid because of the mishap. The similarities end there.

The priest in the Eastern European church slapped the altar boy across the face, screaming and calling him a clumsy oaf and ordering him to leave the altar. That boy left and never set foot in the church again. He grew up to become an atheist and a Communist. His name was Josip

Broz Tito, the strongman dictator of Yugoslavia from 1943 to 1980.

The priest in the church in Illinois dropped down on one knee to get eye level with the altar boy and said, "It's all right, son, you'll do better next time. You'll be a fine priest for God someday." That boy grew up to become the respected and beloved Bishop Fulton J. Sheen.

Two similar experiences with radically different endings; and all because someone spoke the powerful words of encouragement and someone else did not. Just say the words. In the spirit of Christ, just say the words of empathy, of love, of encouragement; and healing will come. If we will just say the words, God will do the rest. He will bring the healing.

How are you doing with this? Do you speak the words that build up or the words that tear down? At the end of the day, how will you be remembered? Will you be remembered as one who knew the power of words and used that power well?

—◦❦11❦◦— Will You Be Remembered . . .

As One Who Knew "That Great Gettin' Up Mornin' "?

Scripture: John 11:38-44

We in the church have loved to sing our faith from the very beginning. And with good reason: We have a faith worth singing about!

I don't know about you, but I love the different kinds and varieties of faith music. I love the majestic anthems of Bach and the gospel songs of Fannie Crosby. I love the exuberant music of Mozart and the powerful hymns of Charles Wesley. I love Handel's *Messiah* and Newton's "Amazing Grace." I love camp songs and folk songs and French carols.

However, the most moving and powerful expressions of faith music are found in those great and poignant spirituals that come out of African American culture. Often written in painful and debilitating circumstances, the spirituals cover the full range of human emotions—joy and sorrow, confidence and despair, praise and lament, victory and defeat—but always there is the dominant and recurring theme of eternal hope:

Things may be hard now,
Times may be tough now,
But ultimately God will win,
And if we remain faithful,
He will share his victory with us!

In spirituals, we hear many crucial ideas repeated dramatically. For example, we hear the "good news of Jesus Christ" proclaimed and celebrated like this:

> Go, tell it on the mountain,
> over the hills and everywhere;
> go, tell it on the mountain,
> that Jesus Christ is born.

("Go, Tell It on the Mountain")

And we hear the challenge of discipleship:

> This little light of mine,
> I'm going to let it shine,
>
> . . . .
>
> Let it shine, let it shine, let it shine.

("This Little Light of Mine")

* * * *

I'm gonna sing when the Spirit says sing,
I'm gonna shout when the Spirit says shout,
I'm gonna pray when the Spirit says pray,
And obey the Spirit of the Lord.

("I'm Gonna Sing")

We find also in the spirituals a strong reliance on the comforting presence of Christ in times of trouble:

> Nobody knows the trouble I see,
> Nobody knows but Jesus . . .

("Nobody Knows the Trouble I See")

* * * *

> I want Jesus to walk with me . . .
> In my trials . . .
> When my heart is almost breaking . . .
> When I'm troubled . . .
> When my head is bowed in sorrow,
> Lord, I want Jesus to walk with me.

("I Want Jesus to Walk with Me")

But most of all, in these amazing spirituals we find the hope of Resurrection, the strong belief that death is victory, that death is not death at all; it's going home to be with God. Look at these words to the hymn "Soon and Very Soon":

> No more weepin' and a-wailin'
> Going home to live with God.

(Andraé Crouch, "Soon and Very Soon" [Nashville: Communiqué Music & Crouch Music Group, 1978])

* * * *

> In that great gettin' up mornin',
> Fare thee well, fare thee well.

("In That Great Gettin' Up Mornin'")

* * * *

> Swing low, sweet chariot,
> Coming for to carry me home.

("Swing Low, Sweet Chariot,")

Over and over in these African American spirituals, we hear this powerful theme of Resurrection. Death is not the end, but the beginning. Death is nothing to be afraid of; it is merely a door through which we pass to move into a deeper and more meaningful relationship with God. For the people of faith, death is a victorious "homegoing"! It's going home to be with God. This is the good news of Easter, isn't it?

But we do not have to wait till we die; eternal life can begin for you and me now. Resurrection can happen for you and me *now*. New life is available for you and me right now. We do not have to wait until we physically die to be at home with God. Now, please do not misunderstand me. I believe in that "Great Gettin' Up Mornin'" off in the future, but I also believe that God can raise us up now, that God has the power to bring us out of those dark and dismal tombs now that imprison us and enslave us and smother the very life out of us.

🔊 *"That Great Gettin' Up Mornin'"*

Let me ask you something. Do you feel trapped right now? Do you feel imprisoned, paralyzed, shackled, buried by some problem? Do you feel locked up in some spiritual grave? Is there something in your life right now that is smothering you to death, sapping your strength, depleting your energy, destroying your soul? Is it some weakness? Is it an addiction? Is it an emptiness within? Is it remorse over some wrong that you have done or something you have failed to do? Is it guilt or shame or vengeance? Is it a heavy burden or a secret sin or a sorrow that's covering you like a heavy blanket? Do you feel trapped in some desolate and dreary tomb?

If so, I have good news: God has a resurrection for you! He wants to bring you out into the light again. He wants to bring you out of that tomb and give you a new start. And listen! He has the power to do it. He can bring you back to life. This powerful story in John 11 speaks to this. Remember it with me.

Mary and Martha, who lived in Bethany, were some of Jesus' closest friends. They sent word to him that their brother, Lazarus, was desperately ill. "Please come. We need your help. Hurry. He is sinking fast." But by the time Jesus got there, Lazarus had died and had been in his grave for four days. Mary and Martha came out to meet Jesus, and they expressed their grief. "He's gone. We've lost him. O Lord, if only you had been here, our brother would not have died!"

The family and friends gathered, and in their deep sorrow, they began to weep over the loss of their loved one, Lazarus. The heart of Jesus went out to them, and Jesus wept with them. He loved Lazarus, too, and he loved them, and he shared their pain. Jesus went out to the cave-like tomb, and he said to them, "Roll back the stone!" Martha, always the realist and ever ready to speak out, protested: "But Lord, we can't do that! He has been in the grave for four days. By now there will be a terrible odor." Jesus said to her, "Martha, only believe, and you will see the power of God."

So they rolled the stone away, and Jesus cried out in a loud voice, "Lazarus, come out!" And incredibly, miraculously, amazingly, before their very eyes, Lazarus was resurrected! He came out of the tomb. He still had on his grave clothes. His head and feet were still wrapped with mummylike bandages. Jesus then turned to the friends and family and said to them, "Unbind him, and let him go. Unwrap him, and set him free."

In this graphic and dramatic story, three awesome lessons jump out at us. Three great truths emerge that can be so helpful to us today. Let me list them, and we can take a look at them, one at a time:

1. Jesus wept with those he loved—and he still does.
2. Jesus raised people up—and he still does.
3. Jesus included other people in the healing process—and he still does.

First, Jesus Wept with Those He Loved—and He Still Does

John 11:35: It's the shortest verse in the Bible: "Jesus wept" (RSV). That verse served me well when I was a little boy in Sunday school. Back then, if you could quote a verse of Scripture, you would get a gold star by your name on a big chart. This was my star-producing verse! "Anybody know a verse of Scripture this morning?" the teacher would say, and my hand would go up immediately. "John 11:35: Jesus wept." The next Sunday, the same thing would happen. "Anybody ready to quote a verse of Scripture?" Up went my hand. "John 11:35: Jesus wept." Another gold star. After several Sundays of this, the teacher finally asked, "Jim, do you know any verse other than John 11:35, 'Jesus wept'?"

A few years ago, a young ministerial student was working at our church as a summer intern. He went over to the chapel one Sunday morning to serve Holy Communion. He had never served Communion alone before, and he was scared. Back then, we had the Communion ritual printed on a laminated card. It started with the Invitation to Communion, followed by the Prayer of Confession and the Prayer of Consecration. Just before the people would come forward to receive Communion, the minister would stand, face the congregation, and say, "Hear these words of comfort from the Scriptures . . ." We left a blank there on the Communion card so the minister in charge could at that point quote a favorite verse.

When they got to this point in the service, the young ministerial student stood and said, "Hear these words of comfort from the Scriptures . . ." and then went blank. There was a long pause, and he blurted out the only verse he could think of at the moment: "Jesus wept"! Later, he told me what had happened and how awful he had felt about that at first. But he also told me how one of our members had come down after the service and said to him, "When you quoted that verse, 'Jesus wept,' that was so meaningful to me because it made me suddenly realize that the Healer of our pain is the Feeler of our pain!"

There is a minister serving in Virginia named Al
Hanner. Al Hanner tells a powerful story about his early
days in the ministry. Al says he came out of seminary ready
to be a "Super Preacher." Single-handedly, he would solve
all the problems of the world. He had been trained, he was
well prepared, and now, as a pastor in a little community
in Virginia, he was ready to be a "Super Preacher." He had
all the answers, and he was ready to spout them to the
world with pious religious authority. And that he did, as
the months passed quickly into years.

Then one morning, the phone rang. The father of his
board chairman had died unexpectedly. As Al started to
the family's home, it hit him: *I don't know what to do. I'm
their pastor, and I'm scared. I don't know what to say to
them.* He tried to remember his classes in pastoral care. He
tried to recall appropriate Scripture passages to quote. He
tried to think of some profound theological message to
give these people in their shocked hour of need. He plot-
ted his strategy. *I know what I'll do. I'll go in boldly and
take charge. I'll gather all the family in the living room
and quote the Twenty-third Psalm. That's what I'll do,*
thought Al Hanner. *That's the answer!*

But there was one thing Al Hanner had not counted on.
When he got to the home and gathered the family in the
living room, he looked at their faces, and their pain
became his pain. He suddenly realized how much he loved
these wonderful people, and his heart broke with them. He
was overcome with emotion. He tried to quote the
Twenty-third Psalm, beginning, "The Lord is my shep-
herd." But Al Hanner exploded into tears. He cried so
hard that the family had to rush over and minister to him.

They helped him over to the couch, mopped his brow with a cold cloth, and brought him a glass of water.

Al Hanner was so embarrassed, so ashamed. He felt that he had failed miserably. He was humiliated. He got through the funeral and went immediately to the bishop and asked to be moved to another church. Shortly after, Al was transferred. Several years passed, and each year at annual conference, Al would hide from that family. He could not face them. But one evening he came around a corner, and there they were. He could not avoid them this time. He could not hide.

Their faces lit up when they saw Al. They ran to him and hugged him warmly. "Oh, Al," they said, "we are so glad to see you! Our family loves you. We appreciate you so much. We miss you. We talk about you all the time. We have loved all of our pastors, but you are the one who helped us the most." "Oh, really?" Al asked with genuine surprise. "Oh, yes!" they said. "We'll never forget how you came and cried with us when Daddy died."

There's an important lesson here: When people are in grief, they do not want theological pronouncements. They just want us to come and love them. They just want us to come and cry with them. Jesus wept with those he loved—and he still does. He hurts with us. He feels our pain. We all face suffering some time, and when it comes, we can know that our Lord is hurting with us and that he will love us through it. He will walk through the valley with us, and in time he will bring us out of the valley of sorrow to the mountaintop on the other side. Jesus wept with those he loved—and he still does.

Second, Jesus Raised People Up—and He Still Does

The noted minister Dr. D. L. Dykes said that when he was a student pastor just starting out in the ministry, he wanted to learn how to do things right. So each time he was called on to do something new, he would go to the Bible and find out how Jesus performed that ministerial task, and he would learn from him. All went well until Dr. Dykes was called on to do his first funeral. He turned to the New Testament, only to discover that Jesus performed no funerals, only resurrections!

In John 11, Jesus resurrects Lazarus. He raises him up and brings him out of the tomb. "Lazarus, come out!" he says. See how personal this is! Jesus calls him by name. Now, if you will listen carefully, you can hear Jesus calling *your* name. He has a resurrection for you. He wants to bring you out of that tomb—whatever it is—that is imprisoning you. He wants to set you free. And he has the power to do it. If you will hear his call and respond in faith, he will raise you up and give you a new start, a new chance, a new life.

Jesus wept with those he loved—and he still does. Jesus raised people up—and he still does.

Third and Finally, Jesus Included Other People in the Healing Process—and He Still Does

Don't miss this now. Notice what happens when Lazarus comes out of the tomb. Jesus turns to his family and friends and says, "Unbind him, and let him go. Unwrap him, and set him free." It's amazing to me that some people think the small-group movement is a new thing. Small groups, support groups, are as old as the Bible, and they are so essential. Jesus knew how important it is to have our family and our friends helping us, surrounding us with love, supporting us, encouraging us, setting us free—in every moment, but especially in those dramatic moments when we are trying to make a new start with our lives.

Recently, a man stopped by to see me. A little over a year ago, he went through a great personal tragedy, but he is coming through it with the help of God and with the help of the church, especially his Sunday school class. He said, "I was devastated. I was disillusioned and defeated and saw no hope for the future and no relief for my pain. I was so hurt that I was immobilized. All the life had drained out of me, but God brought me back to life, and this church has been there for me every step of the way. My Sunday school class has been incredible. I don't know what I would have done without them. I couldn't have made it without them."

You know what he was saying, don't you? He was saying, "God brought me out of the tomb, and my friends helped me and supported me, and together, by the grace of God, they loved me back to life.

Jesus wept with those he loved—and he still does. He raised people up—and he still does. He included others in the healing process—and he still does.

Well, what do you think? When your days on this earth are completed, will you be remembered as one who knew about and was ready for "That Great Gettin' Up Mornin'"?

—◌12◌— Will You Be Remembered . . .

As One Who Knew How to Be Beautifully Extravagant?

Scripture: John 12:1-8

Recently I heard a story about a man living in New York City who was kidnapped a few years ago. His kidnappers called his wife and asked for $100,000 ransom. She talked them down to $30,000. The story had a happy ending: The man returned home unharmed, the money was recovered, and the kidnappers were caught and sent to jail. But don't you wonder what happened when the man went home and found that his wife got him back for a discount?

A journalist wrote about this incident. He imagined what the negotiations must have been like: "$100,000 for that old guy? You've got to be crazy. Just look at him. Look at that gut! You want $100,000 for that? You've got to be kidding. Give me a break. $30,000 is my top offer." A pastor illustrated his sermon with this story and added this thoughtful comment: "I suppose there are some here this morning who can identify with the wife in the story, but for some reason I find myself identifying with the husband. I'd like to think if I were in a similar situation, there would be people who would spare no expense to get me back. They wouldn't haggle over the price. They wouldn't say: 'Well, let me think about it!' I like to think that they would say, 'We'll do anything for you.'" The point of that story is this: Sometimes it's okay to be extravagant.

That is precisely what this story in John 12:1-8 is all about. Remember the story with me.

Jesus was on his way to the cross. It was six days before Passover. The Crucifixion was less than a week away, and he knew it. He stopped in Bethany to visit with his good friends, Mary and Martha and Lazarus. Just a few days before, Jesus had raised Lazarus from the dead, and now they all were sitting down to have dinner together. And Mary did a beautiful but extravagant thing for Jesus. She knelt before him, anointed his feet, generously pouring out costly perfumed oil on them, and wiped and dried Jesus' feet with her hair.

Why did she do that? Some say it was an act of gratitude in which she was thanking Jesus for raising her brother, Lazarus, from the dead. Some say it was an act of consecration in which she was baptizing the feet of Jesus to encourage him to go into the Holy City and do what had to be done. Others say it was an act of preparation, in which she was anointing his body for the death that was to come in Jerusalem a few days later. All say that it was an act of love and kindness. But the story does not end there. Mary, after doing this beautiful thing, is reprimanded by Judas for being so wasteful. And Judas is in turn reprimanded by Jesus for being so stingy.

Stinginess means being overly concerned about money, just like the kidnapped man's wife, who obviously felt that money was real important. Maybe she reasoned like this: "Which is easier to replace, a husband or $100,000?" That is stingy thinking, pecuniary thinking, materialistic thinking.

That's the way Judas thought: *What a waste! Look what we could have done with all the money received from selling that perfumed oil. Think of how many poor people we could have fed.* Judas did not intend to sell the oil. (It wasn't even his oil.) It sounded good, and Judas was probably surprised and taken aback when Jesus rebuked him.

The point of the story is simply this: Sometimes it's okay to be extravagant. Sometimes, in the name of love and kindness and gratefulness, it's okay—indeed, it's beautiful—to be extravagant. Let me show you what I mean.

First of All, It's Okay to Be Extravagant in Our Generosity

That's what Mary was doing. It was a beautiful act of sacrificial generosity. Speaking of generosity, I have a friend who is a "reverse tither." She lives on 10 percent of her income and gives away 90 percent to worthy causes, to her church and to Methodist schools and colleges and orphanages and hospitals. She is extravagant in her generosity, and she is one of the happiest persons I know.

Some years ago, there was a small tribe of Native Americans living in the state of Mississippi. They lived along the banks of a very swift and dangerous river. The current was so strong that if somebody accidentally fell in, they would likely be swept away to their death downstream. One day, this tribe was attacked by another tribe.

They found themselves literally with their backs up against the treacherous river. They were greatly outnumbered. Their only chance for escape was to cross the current, which would mean death for the children, the elderly, the weak, the ill, the injured, and likely many of the strong.

The leaders of the tribe devised a plan. The logical thing, the reasonable thing, the expedient thing, the sensible thing was to leave the weak ones behind. They were going to be killed anyway; why risk losing the strong in a futile effort to save the weak? That was the rational answer, but they could not do it. Instead, they chose to be extravagant in their generosity, and they decided that those who were strong would pick up the weaker ones and put them on their shoulders. So the little children, the elderly, and those who were ill or wounded were carried on the backs of the stronger tribe members.

With great fear, they waded out into the rapid waters of the river, and they were met with a great surprise. To their astonishment, they discovered that the weight on their shoulders enabled them to keep their footing through the treacherous current and to make it safely to the other side. Their own extravagant generosity saved them. What they did was not the reasonable thing to do, but it was the right thing to do. The point is that if you, who are strong and comfortable and well fed, will reach out in generosity and help somebody in need, you will be surprised to discover that the life you save may also be your own.

With words and actions, Jesus taught us that sometimes it's okay to be extravagant in our generosity.

Second, It's Okay to Be Extravagant in Our Gratitude

Maybe that's what Mary was doing that day in Bethany—expressing her indescribable thanksgiving to Jesus. Sometimes words just are not enough, and perhaps this extravagant act was her way of trying to say "thank you" to her Lord for all that he had done for them and for the recent act of calling her brother, Lazarus, out of the grave.

Recently, I ran across a wonderful story about a woman who was known far and wide for her grateful spirit. Even when she was diagnosed with a terminal illness and told that she had only three months to live, still she maintained that twinkle in her eye, that terrific sense of humor, and that radiant spirit of gratitude. She went to see her pastor to plan her memorial service, and with a laugh, she told him, "Don't make this a somber or sad occasion, or I'll come back to haunt you! I've had a great life, and I am so thankful for so many things. So let's concentrate on making this a celebration of my life in this world and the next."

Together, she and her pastor selected the hymns and the Scriptures, and then she said, "Oh, yes, there's one more thing. I want to help you with your message." "How's that?" asked the minister. And she said, "I want to be buried with a fork in my right hand!" The pastor blanched a bit, and the woman said, "Are you shocked by that request?" "Curious," replied the minister.

The woman explained, "In all my years in the church, I have attended so many eating meetings—dinners, brunches, luncheons, potluck suppers—and my favorite part was when they were clearing the tables after the main course, and someone would lean over and say, 'You can keep your fork.' That was my favorite part, because I knew that meant that something better was coming! I was so grateful for what I had already had, and now something better was coming! So, when people come to the funeral home and see me there, they are going to say, 'What's with the fork? What's with the fork?' And then at the service you can get up and tell my story, and you can tell them for me that I am so grateful for what I've already had, but I'm keeping my fork because I know that something even better is coming!"

Let me ask you something: Do *you* have that kind of victorious spirit? Do you have that kind of deep faith? Do you have that kind of extravagant gratefulness? If not, why not? Jesus taught us that it's okay to be extravagant in our generosity and in our gratitude.

Third and Finally, It's Okay to Be Extravagant in Our Graciousness

One thing is clear: Whatever meaning scholars may attach to Mary's act of anointing the feet of Jesus with precious oil and then drying his feet with her hair, it was without question an act of love and kindness and graciousness.

Let me tell you about Noel, a minister in Mississippi. He grew up on a farm in the Mississippi Delta, in a family very much like the Walton family from television. All the members of the family would work hard on the farm during the week, and on Saturday, they would pile in the truck and drive into the nearby town to shop and visit and relax. In town, they would split up and go their separate ways and then meet back at the truck at five o'clock to make the three-mile trip back home to the farm.

One Saturday, when Noel was sixteen, he met some of his school friends in town. They wanted him to stay in town and go with them to a basketball game that night. Noel met his family and asked permission to stay in town for the basketball game. After he assured his parents that he could catch a ride home after the game, they agreed to let him stay. However, when the game was over, Noel could not find anybody going his way, so he had no other choice but to walk home, three miles in the dark.

Noel started out walking briskly, then trudgingly, along the gravel road. He had gone about a mile when he heard a noise behind him. It was a car. He waved the car down to hitch a ride. But when he opened the door and the interior lights came on, Noel almost fainted because the driver of the car was Mr. Jim. Now, Mr. Jim was the "town character"—mean and tough, with a sour look and an evil eye—and all the young people and most of the adults of that community were scared to death of Mr. Jim. Mr. Jim lived all alone, had no friends, and was angry and surly and grumpy most all the time. He was, without question, the "town grouch," and everyone went out of his or her way to steer clear of Mr. Jim.

But Noel was committed. So, quaking with fear, he got into the car and with a trembling, squeaking voice said, "Thanks for stopping, Mr. Jim." Mr. Jim grunted and scowled. They rode along in silence. In a scant few minutes (which seemed like an eternity to Noel), they came to Noel's house. As Noel got out of the car, he said, "Thanks a lot for the ride, Mr. Jim." Mr. Jim looked at him angrily and said, "What do you mean, 'Thanks'? That's mighty poor pay." Noel turned red as Mr. Jim's hostile words seared into his brain. Noel felt as if he had been slapped across the face. "I'm sorry, Mr. Jim," Noel stammered. "I don't have any money, but I do want to say thanks for the ride." Mr. Jim looked at him with an icy stare, and he snarled, "I said, what do you mean, 'Thanks'? That's mighty poor pay!" Noel was even more hurt and embarrassed. He got out of the car and ran into the house as his eyes filled with tears. It was one of those awful, painful moments in life that you feel you can never get over or forget. Noel dreaded seeing Mr. Jim even more after that, and he avoided him as much as he could. But when he did see him, the pain, the hurt, the embarrassment would come back.

A few years later, Noel decided to go into the ministry and attended seminary. During his sophomore year, Noel worked odd jobs and saved enough money to buy a car. Then one weekend after midterm exams, Noel decided to go home for a visit. It was dark when he drove through the little town and started down the gravel road toward the farm. About a mile out of town, Noel saw a man on the side of the road waving him down. Noel stopped to pick up the nighttime hitchhiker, and who do you think it was? That's right: Mr. Jim!

Mr. Jim got in, and they rode along in silence. They passed by Noel's house and drove down the road two more miles to Mr. Jim's farmhouse. Noel pulled right up to the front porch. As Mr. Jim started to get out of the car, he turned back and said, "Thanks a lot for the ride, Noel." Now, you know what Noel wanted to say. He wanted to say, "What do you mean, 'Thanks'? That's mighty poor pay." That's what Noel wanted to say. That's what he almost said. Just then the spirit of Christ bubbled up in him, and instead he said, "You're welcome, Mr. Jim, you're welcome! You can ride with me anytime!"

Isn't that a great story? It's powerful because it reminds us in a dramatic way that the Spirit of Christ can empower us and enable us to be extravagant in our generosity, to be extravagant in our gratitude, and to be extravagant in our graciousness.

At the end of the day, how will you be remembered? Will you be remembered as one who knew how to be beautifully extravagant?

___13___

Will You Be Remembered . . .

As One Who Knew How to Be a Real Friend?

Scripture: Mark 2:1-12

Tim and Kyle were best friends in high school. They were like brothers. They studied together; they played sports together; they double-dated together; they hung out together; they did most everything together.

They first met when they were going through the difficult early days of freshman year. It was a Friday afternoon, and Kyle was walking home from school. He was carrying all of his books home. Tim saw him and wondered why in the world anyone would bring all of his books home on a Friday. *He must really be a nerd!* Tim thought. Tim already had a big weekend planned—parties and a football game with his friends set for Saturday afternoon—and studying was not in the picture at all for Tim that weekend.

Just then, Tim saw some older kids pointing at Kyle and all of his books, and they were laughing at him. Kyle was the new kid at school, and the kids were making fun of him and whispering behind his back and plotting against him. Suddenly, the older guys ran toward Kyle. They banged into him full speed, knocking him flat on his back in the dirt. The books went flying everywhere as the older kids passed by and walked down the sidewalk, laughing and congratulating themselves. Tim saw the whole thing. His heart went out to Kyle. He saw terrible sadness in Kyle's eyes. Tim jogged over to help. "Those guys are jerks," Tim said. "They really need to get a life."

He helped Kyle to his feet and helped him pick up his books, and he asked Kyle where he lived. As it turned out, Tim and Kyle lived on the same street, just a few houses apart, but had not met because until this semester, Kyle had been going to a private school.

Tim and Kyle liked each other immediately. They talked all the way home as they each carried an armful of Kyle's books. Tim invited Kyle to play football the next day with him and his friends. Kyle said yes, and a great friendship began. They hung out together all weekend long and found that they shared much in common, and they became real buddies.

On Monday morning, Tim showed up at Kyle's door and said, "I thought I'd better help you with all those books, so people won't think you are a nerd." Kyle smiled. It was one of those smiles that showed real gratitude. He handed over half of his books to Tim, and off they went to school.

Over the next four years, Tim and Kyle became the best of friends. Kyle won an academic scholarship to Georgetown University, and Tim won an athletic scholarship to Duke. Kyle planned to become a doctor; Tim was going to study business. Kyle was valedictorian of their class; Tim teased him all the time about being so smart. Kyle had to prepare a speech for graduation; Tim was glad it was Kyle giving the speech and not him.

On graduation day, Tim saw Kyle getting ready for his speech. Kyle looked great. He really found himself and blossomed during high school. He filled out, became handsome, and everybody at school really liked him now. Tim could see that Kyle was nervous about his speech, so Tim patted him on the back and said, "Hey, Big Guy, this is a piece of cake for you. You'll be great!"

Kyle looked at Tim with a grateful nod. He smiled and said, "Thanks." When Kyle went to the lectern to give his valedictory speech, he cleared his throat and began, "Graduation is a time to thank those who helped us make it through these tough years. Our parents, our teachers, our siblings, our coaches, but mostly, our friends. I am here to tell all of you that being a friend to someone is the best gift you can give them." Then Kyle said, "I am going to tell you a story. But first I want to ask my friend, Tim, to stand up."

Tim nervously stood, listening in amazement as Kyle told the story of how they had first met, of how Tim had come to help him after the big guys had knocked him down. Kyle continued, "Tim is my best friend. He knows everything about me, except one thing. He doesn't know to this day why I was carrying all my books home on Friday afternoon four years ago. You see, I was the new kid in school. I didn't know anybody. I didn't have any friends, and I had gotten depressed. Real depressed. The reason I was carrying all my books home that Friday was because I was planning to take my own life that weekend.

I had cleaned out my locker so my Mom and Dad would not have to do it later, and I was carrying all my stuff home."

Kyle turned to Tim and said, "Tim, I owe you my life. Your friendship saved my life. Your friendship saved me from doing the unspeakable, and I want to say today what I've been waiting four years to say: Thank you! Thank you!" A gasp rippled through the audience as this handsome, popular boy told about his weakest moment and how he was saved by the gift of friendship.

Now, this touching story about the power of friendship reminds me of the Scripture lesson in Mark 2:1-12. Here, we find the touching story of a man whose life, like Kyle's, was turned around in an amazing way because of the love and compassion of his friends. Remember the story with me. It was one of the remarkable events in the ministry of Jesus that was so vivid, so dramatic, and so unforgettable that three of the four Gospel writers included it in their narratives.

In the first chapter of Mark, we see Jesus beginning his ministry. He went through Galilee, preaching, teaching, and healing. Word spread like wildfire about Jesus' eloquent words and power to heal, and people came to seek him out. Jesus came to Capernaum, and a large group of people came to see him and to hear him. They were jammed shoulder to shoulder in the house, at the doors, and looking in the windows, a huge throng of people, a solid mass of humanity. They were listening to Jesus speak when they heard a noise above them.

They looked up, and—imagine their amazement!—they saw the roof open and a man who was paralyzed lowered on his pallet down into the presence of Jesus. Four of the man's friends had brought him to Jesus. They could not get into the house the regular way, so they had lowered him down to the Master through the roof. The people were astonished, but Jesus showed no surprise. In fact, he liked it. He was touched by the love, the ingenuity, and the stubborn faith of these four friends who would not be denied. They so loved their friend who was paralyzed, and they so believed in Jesus' power to help him that they would not quit. They had found a way to get it done.

Jesus' heart went out to them, and he said to the man on the pallet, "Son, your sins are forgiven. Stand up, take up your mat, and walk." And the man did! End of story? Did they all live happily ever after? No, not quite. The scribes and the Pharisees were upset with Jesus. They murmured in the background, talking behind his back and plotting against him.

Isn't this a great story? Many things could be noted and examined here. For example, we could look at the relationship between forgiveness and healing. Why, for example, did Jesus say, "Son, your sins are forgiven," as he healed the man?

Or we could look at Jesus' special way of handling interruptions. He was so good at that.

Or we could look at the conflict between Jesus and the religious authorities of the day. The watchdogs of orthodox religion became so hostile toward Jesus. Why?

All of these are important. But for now, let's zero in on the portrait of Christian love beautifully painted for us by the bold action of these four friends. Look with me at three special ingredients of their love and their friendship.

First of All, They Were Willing to Help

The four friends (don't miss this now!) did not wait to be asked. They were ready. They were willing. They were excited. They were eager to help. As the old saying goes, "That's what friends are for." One of my favorite definitions of *friendship* is the classic statement: "A friend is the one who walks in when all the rest of the world has walked out."

Recently I heard a story about a schoolteacher who decided to travel across America one summer and see the sights she had been teaching about for more than ten years. Traveling alone, she launched out. All went well for several weeks, until a water hose broke in her car's engine, and the engine stalled and then quit. She was stuck on a busy interstate highway in California. She was tired, she was all alone, she was not an auto mechanic, and she was exasperated—and scared! She waved to passing cars for help, but no one would stop. Finally, she gave up, leaned against her car, and prayed: "Please God, send me an angel—preferably one who knows about cars."

About three minutes later, a big man on a Harley-Davidson motorcycle drove up. He was an enormous man with long hair pulled back in a ponytail and tattoos all over his arms. When the schoolteacher saw the biker stopping, she was somewhere between nervous and terrified. He jumped off his cycle and went to work on her car. He went back to his motorcycle and from somewhere pulled out a new water hose. Within minutes, he had her car fixed and running.

The schoolteacher had been too frightened of him to speak. Finally, she got up the courage to say, "Thank you so much," and they had a brief conversation. Noticing her surprise that someone who looked like him could be so nice, he looked her straight in the eyes and said, "Lady, it's best not to judge a book by its cover. I know I don't look like much, but I do know how to be a friend!" With that, he smiled, closed the hood on her car, and jumped on his Harley. With a wave, he was gone as fast as he had appeared.

Let me ask you something. Do you know how to be a friend, how to see someone in need and be there for that person, how to act with compassion and love before you are even asked? That's what the guy on the Harley did. That's what the four friends in Mark 2 did. That's what we as Christians are called to do: to be willing to help.

Second, They Were Willing to Cooperate

The four friends in Mark 2 worked together; they cooperated. How important it is that we in the church learn how to cooperate; we can hurt one another and our cause when we do not. Let me show you what I mean.

Three men were on a fishing trip. Their boat was wrecked in a storm, but they managed to swim to a deserted island. For the first few days, all was well, but after a week, two of the three became despondent. One was a cattle baron from Texas, and he missed his ranch. The second was a cab driver from Manhattan, and he longed to be back in New York in his taxi. The third man was a happy-go-lucky type, and he was rather enjoying himself, finding the experience exciting and fun. One day as they walked together on the beach, they found an ancient lamp. They rubbed the lamp, and a genie sprang forth. "For freeing me from my prison," said the genie, "each of you shall receive one wish, but one wish only."

"I'd sure like to be back on my ranch in Texas," the cattle baron said, and *poof!* He was gone. "I'd sure like to be back in my cab in New York," the cab driver said, and *poof!* He was gone. "And what is your wish?" the genie asked the third man. "Gee," he said, "I'm kinda lonely here with the other guys gone. I sure wish they were back here with me." *Poof! Poof!* (*Reader's Digest,* Nov. 1981).

Now, this story shows dramatically how important it is to cooperate. When we think only about ourselves and about what we want, not much gets accomplished, and people get hurt. The four men in the Mark 2:1-12 cooperated, and as a result, they were productive. A great thing happened because these four friends were willing to help and were willing to cooperate.

Third and Finally, They Were Willing to Risk Criticism

Any time we do something good or give leadership or take a stand, we open ourselves to criticism. In October 1997, Leon Hale wrote a column for the *Houston Chronicle* entitled "When Good Deeds Invite Suspicion." He told about going into a pub to find customers griping and groaning and harshly criticizing a man they called "the windshield wiper."

The windshield wiper was an older man who cleaned the windshields of cars and pickup trucks parked in the pub's lot. The customers gossiped about him, fussed about him, and were sure he was up to no good. But he never asked for tips for his work. Customers could not believe that the man was acting out of kindness. So a citizen performing a good deed was judged as a mental case or a troublemaker.

This was precisely what Jesus was talking about in the Beatitudes (see Matthew 5:3-12). He said, "Go out into the world and be peacemakers and do acts of mercy." Then he added a P.S.: "Oh, by the way, when you do this, you may well be persecuted, but do it anyway, and I will be with you."

Remember Nehemiah in the Old Testament. After the exile, he came back to Jerusalem and began to rebuild the walls of the Holy City. As he worked, his enemies taunted him, ridiculed him, and threatened him. But Nehemiah kept working, and he answered, "I'm doing a great work, and I cannot come down" (Nehemiah 6:3). Don't you love that response? "I'm doing a great work, and I cannot come down."

Remember Abraham Lincoln during the American Civil War. He was scathingly criticized, but he was committed to saving the Union and said, "If I were to try to read, much less answer, all the attacks made on me, this shop might as well be closed for any other business. I do the very best I know how . . . ; and I mean to keep doing so until the end. . . . If the end brings me out wrong, ten angels swearing I was right would make no difference" (Francis B. Carpenter, *The Inner Life of Abraham Lincoln: Six Months at the White House* [University of Nebraska Press, 1995], 258-59).

You know what Lincoln was saying, don't you? Like Nehemiah before him, he was saying, "I am doing a great work, and I cannot come down."

In similar fashion, the four friends in Mark 2 were so determined to get their friend into the presence of Jesus that they tore open the roof of the house. They knew they could be criticized for this (these days, they would be sued for millions!), but they did it anyway. They were doing a great work, and they could not come down.

But most important here, look at Jesus. He knew the authorities had their watchdogs there, scrutinizing his every move. He knew that whatever he did, they would find fault and turn it against him. He also knew that this man who was paralyzed was the victim of the bad theology of that day, the bad theology that taught people that all suffering was the consequence of some sin. Jesus refuted that idea and showed us in words—and later, dramatically on a cross—that sometimes in this world, bad things can happen to good people.

But Jesus knew that this man on the pallet probably believed that his paralysis was the consequence of some sin, so he met him where he was and said, "Son, your sins are forgiven. Rise, take up your pallet, and walk." Jesus also knew that these words and these actions would cause trouble with the religious authorities of that time, but Jesus did it anyway, putting love first. Jesus, like the four friends, demonstrates for us the power of love, the power of grace, the power of friendship. Like the four friends, Jesus was willing to help, willing to cooperate, and willing to risk criticism.

You see, that's what real friendship is about, and that's what friends are for. Maybe this is what Joseph Scriven had in mind when he wrote his most famous hymn, "What a Friend We Have in Jesus."

But the question is, at the end of the day, will you be remembered as one who knew the meaning of friendship? And more important, will you be remembered as one who knew how to be a real friend?

—∽14∽—

Will You Be Remembered . . .

As One Who Knew How to Close the Gate?

Scripture: Philippians 3:12-16

Dr. Tom Tewell, who is the pastor of the Fifth Avenue Presbyterian Church in New York, recently told about a fascinating tradition at Culver Military Academy. At the graduation exercises, the cadets, one by one, walk across the stage, receive their diplomas from the dean, shake hands with the president, and walk through an archway into their future. They are told as they walk through the archway, "Don't forget to close the gate." The purpose of that command is not just a matter of military neatness, but rather a symbolic acting out of this message: "Close the gate on your past mistakes and failures and sins before walking into your future."

It's a great parable for us, isn't it? Each morning as we step out into a new day, there are some things we need to close the gate on. There are some things we need to forget before we can move on with our lives.

Now, we like to joke about our memories and especially our forgetfulness. The old vaudeville comedians had a good time with this. For example, remember the joke about the man who came to his doctor and said, "Doc, I have a terrible memory; I can't remember anything." The doctor said, "How long have you had this problem?" And the man said, "What problem?" And then there's the joke where the man comes to his doctor and says, "Doctor, I have a terrible memory, what should I do?" And the doctor said, "Pay me in advance!"

Let's take some time now to think about a good kind of forgetfulness, the kind of forgetfulness that empowers us to close the gate on the skeletons of the past, so that we can move creatively and unencumbered into our future.

The power to forget some things is so crucial. With that in mind, consider these two vignettes.

Two men were talking one day. The first man said, "You know, I have a friend who has a terrible memory, the worst memory I ever heard of." The second man said, "Forgets everything, huh?" The first man answered, "No! *Remembers* everything!"

Clara Barton, founder of the American Red Cross, was once reminded of a cruelty done to her. She said serenely, "I distinctly remember forgetting that!" The great people have always known that there are some things we are better off to forget.

The apostle Paul knew how to "close the gate" and move on. In his letter to the Philippians, he put it like this: "Forgetting those things that are past, forgetting what lies behind, I press on" (Philippians 3:14). Paul had learned that as wonderful as it is to remember, it is also good sometimes to forget. It is good sometimes to intentionally remember to forget. Now, let me be more specific. Let me underscore some specific things that we need to put behind us and forget, on which we need to close the gate as we move on with our lives.

First of All, We Need to Close the Gate on Our Past Successes

That's a strange thing to say, isn't it? "Forget your successes; forget your past accomplishments." But the truth is that success does ruin some people. They "bask in the glow" of their past victories and become spoiled and lazy and complacent, and they forget their priorities.

Recently, I heard a basketball coach in a postgame interview, after his team had lost in the closing seconds, say this: "We couldn't stand success out there tonight. We got ahead and got cocky. We got a good lead, and then we just quit. We lost our concentration. We lost our intensity. We became lackadaisical and sloppy. We lost our focus and abandoned our game plan. Our early success ruined us, and once again, we did it—we snatched defeat from the jaws of victory." That's a pretty good parable for life, isn't it? Our own successes can do us in, if we are not careful. Our own successes can make us lazy and spoiled and complacent if we dwell on our past accomplishments and forget to give our energies to the present.

The Dallas Cowboys learned this lesson the hard way on January 2, 1999. They played the Arizona Cardinals in one of the first wild-card games of the National Football League playoffs. Dallas was a heavy favorite to win. They were expected to win because they had won so many playoff games before, and indeed, several Super Bowls. The Cardinals, on the other hand, had not won a playoff game since 1947. That was the year Chuck Yeager broke the sound barrier, Jackie Robinson integrated baseball, and Harry Truman became the first president to address the nation on television. That's how long it had been since the Cardinals had won a playoff game. In addition, the Cowboys had beaten the Cardinals sixteen out of the last seventeen times and twice that season. All true but absolutely meaningless because you don't play the game in the past; you play it in the present. And against all odds, on January 2, 1999, the young, upstart, inexperienced Arizona Cardinals beat the mighty Dallas Cowboys, 20 to 7.

Now, there is a sermon there somewhere, and maybe it is the message that our past successes can immobilize us if we dwell on them too much. I don't know a lot about boxing, but I know enough to understand two phrases that boxing analysts use, phrases that carry over into other dimensions of life. I recently heard a former boxer talking on television about an upcoming fight, and he used these two phrases. He predicted that one fighter, who had been very successful as a boxer, would lose because (here is the first phrase), he said, "He has become a fat cat." And he predicted the other boxer would win because (here is the second phrase), he said, "He is a hungry fighter."

Although I'm not an expert on boxing, I knew what he was talking about. "Fat cats" in any field are those who, because of their past successes, have become spoiled, lazy, complacent, self-satisfied, pompous, prideful, prima donnas, whereas those who are "hungry" are those in any field who are striving, stretching, struggling, working, dreaming, reaching, sacrificing—those willing to pay the price.

As I thought of this, my mind darted back to one of the Beatitudes of Jesus: "Blessed are those who hunger and thirst for righteousness" (Matthew 5:6). And I also thought back to our Scripture for this chapter—Paul's words to the Philippians—"Forgetting what lies behind . . . I press on." The point is clear: As individual Christians and as a church, we have to constantly guard against the temptation to become "fat cats." We have to stay hungry!

We cannot relax and rely on our press clippings. We must not rest on our laurels. We dare not dwell on our past accomplishments. No wonder Paul resolved to forget his earlier achievements. He knew that there was a new challenge, a new opportunity in the present. And he calls upon us to forget what lies behind and press on into the future and close the gate on our past successes.

Second, We Need to Close the Gate on Our Past Hurts

We need to forget and move beyond those past hurts that dampen our spirits, drain our energies, and poison our souls.

Dr. Paul Tournier, in his book entitled *A Doctor's Case Book in the Light of the Bible* (New York: Harper & Row, 1976), tells of treating a woman for anemia. He had been working with her for several months without much success. He had tried all kinds of medicines, vitamins, and diet and exercise, but all to no avail. There was no improvement at all. He decided to put her in the hospital as a last resort. However, as she was checking in, the hospital checked her blood as part of a routine. They discovered that it was fine. She was well, with no sign of anemia.

Dr. Tournier checked her with the same results. She was healed miraculously. Intrigued by this, Dr. Tournier asked, "Has anything out of the ordinary happened in your life since I saw you last?" "Yes," she said, "I forgave someone against whom I had borne a nasty grudge for a long time. We reconciled. We are friends again. I felt I could at last say 'Yes' to life."

You see, her past hurt, and her seething about and agonizing over it, had made her ill. When she forgave the person who hurt her, when that reconciliation came, the impact was so great, so powerful, that it literally and dramatically changed the physical state of her blood and made her well.

Wow! What a message is wrapped up in that story! What a crucial lesson for life is found here! Don't let your past hurts immobilize you! Don't let past hurts fester within you! Don't let past hurts make you sick!

Go fix that! Go get reconciled! Go "close that gate"!

The apostle Paul said, "Forget about your hurts. Don't nurse grievances! Don't give in to self-pity! Put them behind you, and go on with life!" We can close the gate on our past successes and on our past hurts.

Third and Finally, We Need to Close the Gate on Our Past Failures

Remember Frank Sinatra singing the song about picking yourself up, dusting yourself off, and starting all over again ("Pick Yourself Up," 1936). That's a nice song, and a good thought, but the truth is that we need help with that. We cannot really do that by ourselves.

God is the One who can pick us up and dust us off and give us a new start. That's why Jesus Christ came into the world: to give us forgiveness, a new chance, a new start, and a new beginning, and to close the gate on our past sins and failures.

Several years ago, a newspaper reporter interviewed one of the country's best-known psychologists. The reporter asked, "What do you do for those who come to you for treatment?" The noted psychologist answered, "Our objective is to free the patient from the tyranny of the past."

How important that is! All of us have a past that haunts us. All of us have known painful failure. We have all made mistakes. We have all fallen short. We have all short-cut our best selves. We have all sinned. We all need to be set free from the tyranny of the past.

In Garrison, New York, the Walter Hoving Home is dedicated to helping young women close the gate on their sordid pasts and make a new start with their lives. Many of the women they help have been prostitutes in New York City, and most all of them have been drug addicts. The first day they arrive at the home, they are asked to sit down in front of a computer screen, and on the screen appear these words: "Welcome, [Ruthie or Brenda or Patsy, or whatever the individual's name may be], welcome to the first day of the rest of your life."

Then the computer instructs the young women to type all the things they are sorry for—all their sins, all their mistakes, all their failures. It takes them hours (and some of them, several days) to complete the list of all their past wrongdoings.

The young women are told to take the Bible on the desk and turn to Jeremiah 31:34-35 and to type that verse on the computer screen under their list of past sins. That verse says: "I will forgive their iniquity, and remember their sin no more. Thus says the LORD" (vv. 34-35*a*).

Then the computer instructs the young women to press the delete key; and as they do this, the list of sins is wiped away, gone forever, erased completely, blotted out.

They are instructed to type Jeremiah 31:34-35 again: "I will forgive their iniquity, and remember their sin no more. Thus says the LORD."

These words appear on the computer screen: "If God has forgiven it, why don't you?"

Wouldn't that be something—to have a spiritual delete key! Well, the truth—the good news—is that we have it. Through Jesus Christ, we have it. It's called amazing grace, divine forgiveness. It's called redemption, atonement, reconciliation, new life in Christ. It helps so much to know that, with the help of Christ, we can have new life and we can close the gate on our past successes, on our past hurts, on our past failures.

That's a key to meaningful living, isn't it? Have you discovered it? At the end of the day, will you be remembered as one who knew how to close the gate?

Epilogue

Making Every Day Count!

This is the day that the LORD *has made; / let us rejoice and be glad in it. (Psalm 118:24)*

Let me ask you a personal question: Are you making every day count for something? Are you really living life to the full? Are you really celebrating life? Do you see each day as a special gift from God—exhilarating; exciting; packed with fresh, new possibilities, with unique opportunities? Or is life passing you by? What *will* people say about you at the end of the day?

Sadly, it is a well-documented fact that many people today are indeed unhappy and unfulfilled in the present moment. They are so caught up in looking to another day that they miss the joy and meaning of *this* day. To some, the good days are way back there in the past. Others long for better days off in the future. Still others are harried and frustrated and depleted by the pressure-packed busyness of hectic modern-day living. And all of these people are missing real life! They are not really living. They are coping, surviving, "hanging in there," but not really celebrating life! Well, be honest now: How is it with you? Are you really living or is life passing you by?

I ran across an editorial about this that is worth sharing. It was entitled "A Gift from God: Let Life Surround You Each Day." Here is part of it:

Some people call it "the glooms." For the older generation, it's called "the blues." Young folks have still another
name for it . . . that "depressed out of sorts feeling," that
sometimes comes without warning and often without real
reason. A harsh word from the boss, deserved or not, can
produce the glooms. A homemaker overcooks the roast
and slumps into depression. . . .

The glooms can strike suddenly from many different
directions . . .

Psychiatrists offer ways of fighting the glooms; but some
people turn to tranquilizers or alcohol. . . . A simpler and
better remedy is . . . walk outside. Look at the grass and
the trees. Sample the sunlight. Breathe in the air, let life
surround you. Then the soothing realization that each day
is a precious gift from God . . . will easily overwhelm the
glooms.

As I read that editorial, it reminded me of Orville Kelly.
Orville Kelly, a newspaperman from Iowa, went to the
hospital at age forty-three for an examination and was
told he had terminal cancer. Of course, he was stunned by
this devastating news, as was his wife, Wanda. After further hospital tests, the doctors told Orville Kelly that he
had from six months to three years to live. Tension began
to build in the family, while the four children had not been
told what was wrong.

Friends avoided discussing the matter with Orville and
Wanda, simply advising them, "Don't think about it," and
then quickly changing the subject. Communication almost
stopped. Wanda wanted to say something loving, positive,
hopeful, and Orville wanted to reassure her; but neither

could find the simple, honest words, so they remained silent.

Orville Kelly was put on a program of chemotherapy, and the long drive to and from the hospital was a painful, silent journey. One day, Orville said, "Wanda, we have got to talk. I'm not dead yet. Yes, I've got cancer, and yes, I'll probably die from it. But I'm not dead yet, and we've just got to talk about it." And they did—honestly, openly, and lovingly. Then Orville Kelly said, "Let's go home and have a big barbecue, invite all our friends, tell the children about it, and start living again. I don't want to waste any more time this way."

A short time later, a fresh, new, and exciting idea came to Orville Kelly, and he said, "I'm not going to get up in the morning anymore thinking this is one day less to live. Rather, I'm going to take on a new attitude. I'm going to thank God every day for the gift of this day!" And he decided to form a new club called the "MTC"—"Make Today Count!" He said, "After all, everyone is terminal. I simply know that my terminus has been more clearly determined. None of us know for sure when we are going to die. We are all terminal, every last one of us. So, I am going to make every day of my life really count for something wonderful. I'm going to see every day as a special and gracious gift from God."

And that is precisely what he did. And you ought to hear Orville Kelly's description of the mighty Mississippi River on a misty morning or his incredible word picture of a bluebird sitting on the fence of an Iowa farm or his play-by-play description of looking down on Boston through scattered clouds as his plane rose up into the sunlight or his tribute to the smile on his wife's beautiful face. Though sentenced to death by a terminal illness, Orville Kelly actually became more alive by making each day count. (See Norman Vincent Peale, *Creative Help for Daily Living,* Part III [1980], 27-28.)

Isn't this what the psalmist was trying to teach us when he said, "This is the day that the LORD has made; / let us rejoice and be glad in it"? These magnificent words from the psalms have been used for centuries at the opening of lofty worship services as an appropriate call to worship, but they are so much more; they are also practical and dynamic words for daily living.

If you and I could say these words at the beginning of each day and really mean them, it would change our lives: "This is the day that the Lord has made and given to me as a gracious gift; I will rejoice and be glad in it and be thankful for it." Recently, I saw a bumper sticker that says it well: "Today is God's gift to us. That's why it's called 'the present.'" Today is God's day. He has given it to us, and we should see it as a special gift and make it count. To waste it or to corrupt it is sinful and destructive.

Well, how are you doing? Are you really making every day count? Or is life passing you by? As we think this through, let me suggest some ways we can make every day count.

First, We Can Make Every Day Count by Saying, "Today, I Will Be Aware"

"Today, I will be sensitive to what is happening around me, aware of what I am seeing, hearing, and feeling, sensitive to the wonders and challenges of God's world."

ᘒ   *Epilogue*

Out of the Watergate controversy some years ago, a new word came into popular usage. Remember it. The word was *stonewall.* Politically, it meant to "be unaware; act like you've heard nothing, seen nothing, and know nothing." In a sense, that's what many of us do each day. We stonewall! We shut the world out! So many different interest groups, marketing experts, political philosophers, commercial products, and religious gurus scream at us and clamor after us, trying to win our attention, our loyalty, our support, and our money. We are so pushed and pulled, so mesmerized, so inundated that we stonewall the world out and shut our senses down. Like zombies or robots many people move relentlessly through life, unfeeling, untouched, uninspired, unaware.

A few years ago, I was browsing through a magazine and came upon an article that changed my life. It had an "Awareness Test" that was very simple, but it jolted me powerfully. The "Awareness Test" had five simple questions about our five basic senses. It asked,

1. What were the last five sounds you heard?
2. What were the last five sights you saw?
3. What were the last five surfaces you touched?
4. What were the last five fragrances you smelled?
5. What were the last five things you tasted?

I had to work hard at remembering those things. How about you? Could you answer those questions right now?

Isn't it something how we stonewall? We become so insensitive, so unaware of what's happening around us, that we shut down our senses and wall out the world.

I sat down in the grass and took it all in, and it was wonderful. I remembered that verse from psalms, "This is the day that the LORD has made; / let us rejoice and be glad in it"; and I realized, with shame, how rarely I had been doing that. I asked God to forgive me and to help me to be more sensitive, more aware.

We all know of the physical blindness of Helen Keller, but spiritually she had 20/20 vision. Look at her words:

> I have walked with people whose eyes are full of light but see nothing in sea or sky, nothing in city streets, nothing in books. It were far better to sail in the night of blindness with sense, and feeling and mind than to be content with the mere act of seeing. The only lightless dark is the night in ignorance and insensibility.

A good prayer to start each day might well be, "Lord, make me aware today! Give me the eyes of faith!"

Second, We Can Make Every Day Count by Saying, "Today, I Will Do Something Good for Someone Else"

"I will not live today by the code of selfishness; I will not live today by the law of the jungle; I will strike a blow for love today." It's the best therapy in the world. It's the key to happiness—getting outside yourself and thinking about somebody else.

Bishop Bob Goodrich once told the story about a man who knelt at an altar and prayed for a friend, "O Lord, help my friend; help him, Lord, before it's too late. Touch him, Lord, touch him even if just with your finger." Then it was almost as if he heard the voice of God whispering back in his ear, "You touch him; you are my finger."

One of the ways we as Christians make each day count is by reaching out and touching other people in the spirit of Christ. Today, I will be aware. Today, I will do something good for someone else.

Finally, We Can Make Every Day Count by Saying, "Today, I Will Trust God for Tomorrow"

To paraphrase the songwriter, we do not know what the future holds, but we do know who holds the future.

In my study, I have an interesting book. I love the title: *Why Jesus Never Had Ulcers* (Nashville: Abingdon Press, 1986). The author, Robert M. Holmes, a United Methodist minister in Montana, points out that Jesus never had ulcers because he remembered his priorities, that which was important! He remembered his calling to be truthful, not to worry about success. He remembered who was in charge. He remembered to do his best today and to trust God for tomorrow and all the tomorrows of eternity.

That's what it's all about, isn't it? That's how to make each day count. "Today, I will be aware. Today, I will do something good for someone else. And today, I will trust God for tomorrow."

"This is the day that the LORD has made; / let us rejoice and be glad in it."

Suggestions for Leading a Study of *At the End of the Day, How Will You Be Remembered?*

John D. Schroeder

This book by James W. Moore offers insights for making the most of God's gift of life. As a leader, you have the opportunity to help the members of your group become more effective Christians. Here are some suggestions to keep in mind as you begin:

1. You should review the entire book before your first group meeting so that you have an overview of the book and can be a better guide for the members of your group. You may want to use a highlighter to designate important points in the text.

2. Give a copy of the book to each participant before the first session and ask participants to read the introduction before your initial meeting. You may wish to limit the size of your group to ensure that everyone gets a chance to participate. Not everyone may feel comfortable reading aloud, answering questions, or participating in group discussion or activities. Let group members know that this is okay, and encourage them to participate as they feel comfortable doing so.

3. Begin each session by reviewing the main points using the chapter summary. You may ask group members what they saw as highlights. Use your own reading, any notes you have taken, and this study guide to suggest other main points.

4. Select in advance the discussion questions and activities you plan to use. Use those you think will work best with your group. You may want to ask the questions in a different order from the way they are presented in the study guide. Allow a reasonable amount of time for questions and a reasonable amount of time for one or two activities. You may create your own questions and activities if you desire.

5. Before moving from questions to activities, ask members if they have any questions that have not been answered.

6. Following the conclusion of the final activity, close with a short prayer. If your group desires, pause for individual prayer requests.

7. Start your meetings on time and end them on schedule.

8. If you ask a question and no one volunteers an answer, begin the discussion by suggesting an answer yourself. Then ask for comments and other answers.

9. Encourage total participation by asking questions of specific members. Your role is to give everyone who desires it the opportunity to talk and to be involved. Remember, you can always ask such questions as "Why?"

and "Can you explain in more detail?" to continue and deepen a discussion.

10. Be thankful and supportive. Thank members for their ideas and participation.

Introduction: At the End of the Day

Chapter Summary

1. We each leave a legacy when our earthly life is through.

2. Will you be remembered as one who fought the good fight?

3. Will you be remembered as one who finished the race?

4. Will you be remembered as one who kept the faith?

Reflection / Discussion Questions

1. What new insights did you receive from reading this chapter?

2. How easy or difficult is it for you personally to reflect on end-of-life issues? Explain. Has your perspective on this changed—or do you think it could change—over time? If so, how?

3. Briefly name one or two highlights of your life so far.

4. Briefly recall a rough time in your life, and tell what got you through it.

5. How important is your legacy, and why?

6. What types of things do we usually remember about a person who has just died?

7. Describe a deceased family member or acquaintance in a word, phrase, or sentence. Explain your choice of words.

8. List some good things and some bad things that outlast people. Give examples.

9. What things in life are important to you? What gives your life meaning?

10. What did the apostle Paul write for his epitaph?

11. What does it mean to "fight the good fight"?

12. How is the Christian life like a race? What does it mean to "keep the faith"?

Practical Applications / Activities

1. Talk with others you know and seek their opinions on what makes for a meaningful life. Make a list of important ideas from your conversations.

2. In your private time, reflect on this question: As of this moment, how would I be remembered?

3. Be aware of how you use your time this week, keeping track of what is important and what is not.

4. Watch the movie *It's a Wonderful Life*. Reflect on / discuss: What lessons can we learn from this movie that we can apply to our own lives?

5. "At the end of the day, be sure you have done something that outlasts you." Reflect on this statement, and write down some ways in which you might achieve (or already have achieved) this goal.

Prayer: *Dear God, help us take a good look at our lives and realize which things are important and which are not. May we be remembered as examples of your love. Be with us this week. Amen.*

Chapter 1

Will You Be Remembered . . . As One Who Knew Christ's Healing Love?

Chapter Summary

1. Christianity is a lifestyle we live.

2. Christ's healing love gives us a self we can live with.

3. Christ's healing love gives us a faith we can live by.

4. Christ's healing love gives us a love we can live out.

Reflection / Discussion Questions

1. What new insights did you receive from reading this chapter?

2. How do we sometimes misread the signs on life's journey? Give an example.

3. In your own words, explain what happened in Acts 3:1-10.

4. How does the world batter our self-esteem? What wrong messages do we receive?

5. In your own words, explain what "a self we can live with" means.

6. Recall a time when a lie came back to trouble you.

7. What does "a faith we can live by" mean to you?

8. Talk about a time when your faith was put to work or tested.

9. Name a person who has shown you Christ's healing love. Explain how this occurred.

10. What do we need to do to receive Christ's healing love?

11. How has Christ's healing love changed you over the years?

12. How has this discussion / reflection helped or challenged you?

Practical Applications / Activities

1. Discuss some strategies for living your faith or putting your faith to work.

2. List some situations that could use God's healing love.

3. Perform an act of healing love this week.

4. Share with a friend or family member what you learned from this lesson.

5. Spend time in prayer this week, asking God to give you opportunities to share healing love with others. Reflect on how God's love has healed you.

Prayer: *Dear God, thank you for your gift of healing love. May we share this love with others, reaching out to help those in need. Grant us a self that we can live with and a faith that we can live by, along with a love that we can live out. Amen.*

Chapter 2

Will You Be Remembered . . . As One Who Celebrated the Joy of the Journey?

Chapter Summary

1. The real promised lands are within us.

2. Disappointment, frustration, and uncompleted tasks are common to us all.

3. God is with each of us during our journey.

4. Each person dies with something left undone.

Reflection / Discussion Questions

1. What new insights did you receive from reading this chapter?

2. In your own words, explain what it means to celebrate the joy of the journey.

3. Talk about a time when you celebrated the joy of the journey.

4. How do we sometimes miss the joy of the journey?

5. What is a "happy ending" that you are looking forward to reaching eventually?

6. Name some events in life that awaken us to the present joys in life.

7. Talk about something you looked forward to that never materialized. How did it make you feel?

8. Discuss / reflect on this statement: "We can claim the promised land now."

9. According to the author, what "sacred privilege and awesome responsibility" do we carry with us on our Christian journey?

10. "The journey is what counts." Explain what that means to you.

11. In what ways was Jesus' life a journey?

12. How has this discussion / reflection helped or challenged you?

Practical Applications / Activities

1. List some ways in which we can celebrate the joy of the journey.

2. Reflect on or discuss this statement: "We do our best

and trust God for the rest." How does this idea apply in your life?

3. Make specific attempts to "live in the moment" this week. Share your results next week.

4. Discuss with a friend—or make a list of—examples where important work or an important cause was left uncompleted by one generation and passed on to the next. From your examples, what were the consequences, and what were the benefits?

5. Share with a friend or family member what you learned from this lesson.

Prayer: *Dear God, thank you for this wonderful journey we call life. Help us remember that you are with us every step of the journey. Awaken us to present joys and to the love of family and friends. May we celebrate life and your love this week and always. Amen.*

Chapter 3

Will You Be Remembered . . . As One Who Knew the Gift of the Holy Spirit?

Chapter Summary

1. The Holy Spirit redeems situations.

2. The Holy Spirit reminds us of the Truth.

3. The Holy Spirit restores our strength.

4. The Holy Spirit is a gift from God that can turn our lives around.

Reflection / Discussion Questions

1. What new insights did you receive from reading this chapter?

2. What impresses you about the story of John Wesley?

3. What is the gift of the Holy Spirit, and what does it empower us to do?

4. Who do you remember as one who knew the gift of the Holy Spirit? Explain.

5. When did the disciples receive the Holy Spirit? What happened as a result?

6. Explain how the Holy Spirit redeems situations.

7. Talk about a time you asked God to redeem a situation. What were the results?

8. What story in this chapter made an impression on you? Explain.

9. Explain this statement: "Sometimes when we least expect it, the Holy Spirit reveals the truth." How might this have happened at some time in your life?

10. Recall a time when you relied on the Holy Spirit to restore your strength.

11. What do we need to do to receive the gift of the Holy Spirit?

12. How has this discussion / reflection helped or challenged you?

Practical Applications / Activities

1. Look through the Bible to find examples where someone, filled with the power of God, was able to accomplish things that could not be done independent from God.

2. Make a list of the blessings and gifts of the Holy Spirit.

3. Share with a friend or family member something you learned in this lesson.

4. Try your best this week to step back and let God go to work.

5. Discuss / reflect on what has to happen in order for the Holy Spirit to work in us.

Prayer: *Dear God, thank you for the gift of the Holy Spirit. Help us to remember that the Holy Spirit can redeem any situation and restore our strength. May we learn to rely more on you and your love rather than on ourselves. Amen.*

Chapter 4

Will You Be Remembered . . . As One Who Knew How to Trust the Right Things?

Chapter Summary

1. Put your trust in your family.

2. Put your trust in your church.

3. Put your trust in God.

4. Our children are our "early warning signals" for where we are in our culture.

Reflection / Discussion Questions

1. What new insights did you receive from reading this chapter?

2. Talk about a time when you put your trust in the wrong thing or the wrong person.

3. What can help us decide where to place our trust?

4. In your own words, explain why trust is so important.

5. Share a childhood experience in learning about trust.

6. Why did Joshua make his declaration of trust in God? What was the context?

7. What story in this chapter had an impact on you? Explain.

8. Explain this statement: "Our children are our canaries." Do you agree? Why or why not?

9. In what ways can the church serve as your family?

10. What prevents us from putting our trust in God?

11. How can God help us with issues of trust?

12. How has this discussion / reflection helped or challenged you?

Practical Applications / Activities

1. Talk about / reflect on what makes a person trustworthy. Whom do you trust, and why?

2. Make a list of things in general that clamor for our trust and loyalty.

3. Talk about what our children—whether your own or our nation's—are struggling with today. List some of their needs.

4. Reflect or discuss: How did the events of September 11, 2001, touch your life and family and affect your level of trust?

5. Make a mental note this week of how many situations you encounter where you must put your trust in someone or something.

Prayer: _Dear God, thank you for your gift of trust. May we learn to trust you more and always look to you as our primary source of help and strength. Be with us during the coming week. Amen._

Chapter 5

Will You Be Remembered . . . As One Who Knew the Power of Compassion?

Chapter Summary

1. It is possible to be a person with a cold, cold heart.

2. It is possible to be a person with a calculating heart.

3. It is possible to be a person with a compassionate heart.

4. The choice is ours.

Reflection / Discussion Questions

1. What new insights did you receive from reading this chapter?

2. In your own words, explain the meaning of *compassion*.

3. Talk about a time when someone was compassionate toward you.

4. Talk about a time you acted with compassion toward someone.

5. Recall a past encounter with a coldhearted person, or give an example of a coldhearted act.

6. What do you think causes a person to become coldhearted?

7. What impresses you most in the story of the good Samaritan?

8. How can a person be cold, calculating, or compassionate, depending on a specific situation? What factors are involved in how we react to human need?

9. Give an example of how a "respectable" person might sometimes be coldhearted.

10. What's the difference between a person with a cold heart and one with a calculating heart?

11. List some people who are remembered as being compassionate.

12. How has this discussion / reflection helped or challenged you?

Practical Applications / Activities

1. Compassion motivates us to act. Are there times when it is in our best interest not to act? Explain.

2. List and reflect on / discuss some modern-day good Samaritan stories.

3. Perform an act of compassion for a stranger this week.

4. Reflect on / discuss: Are love and compassion the same thing? What are the differences, if any?

5. Reflect on / discuss: What factors cause a person to be compassionate?

Prayer: *Dear God, we thank you for your gift of compassion. May we be remembered as compassionate people and act with compassion toward others. We ask you to provide us with situations where we can show your love. Help us remember your love and that you are always with us. Amen.*

Chapter 6

Will You Be Remembered . . . As One Who Knew How to Teach Children the Key Things in Life?

Chapter Summary

1. Honesty is an enduring value.

2. Love is an enduring value.

3. Faith is an enduring value.

4. Adults need to be role models of faith, love, and honesty for children.

Reflection / Discussion Questions

1. What new insights did you receive from reading this chapter?

2. Who taught you your values as a child?

3. Talk about an early lesson you learned about honesty.

4. Talk about an early lesson you learned about love.

5. Talk about an early lesson you learned about faith.

6. List and reflect on / discuss things that children need to know about honesty.

7. List and reflect on / discuss things that children need to know about love.

8. List and reflect on / discuss things that children need to know about faith.

9. How can adults be good role models for children?

10. How would you explain to a child the meaning of integrity?

11. How can the church play a role in promoting good values in children?

12. How has this discussion / reflection helped or challenged you?

Practical Applications / Activities

1. Reflect on / discuss: Can children pass on good values to other children? To what degree do children influence others? As a child, how were you influenced by other children?

2. Identify negative influences in society that have an impact on children.

3. Brainstorm ideas and strategies for promoting good values.

4. List some obstacles that prevent adults from teaching good values to children. Reflect on / discuss: In what ways are we responsible for all children, regardless of whether we are parents? What benefits does society derive when we adequately meet this responsibility?

5. Locate some Bible stories that teach good values. If

possible, find a way to share one or more of these stories with a child in your life.

Prayer: *Dear God, we are all children in your sight. Help all of us be good role models of honesty, love, and faith to children and to one another. Thank you for your love that empowers us to achieve great things in your name. May we be aware of the importance of all our words and actions this coming week. Amen.*

Chapter 7

Will You Be Remembered . . . As One Who Knew the Importance of Prayer?

Chapter Summary

1. Jesus teaches us to pray in the spirit of gratitude.

2. Jesus teaches us to pray in the spirit of forgiveness.

3. Jesus teaches us to pray in the spirit of trust.

4. Prayer is friendship with God.

Reflection / Discussion Questions

1. What new insights did you receive from reading this chapter?

2. Who taught you the importance of prayer? How did you learn about it?

3. Talk about a key experience you have had with prayer.

4. Why do we sometimes forget or miss the special nature of the Lord's Prayer?

5. What was Christ's purpose in giving us the Lord's Prayer?

6. What motivated the disciples to ask Jesus to teach them about prayer?

7. In your own words, describe what prayer means to you.

8. In your own words, talk about why prayer is so important.

9. What can we learn from the Lord's Prayer?

10. What does it mean to live in a spirit of gratitude?

11. Why is it important to pray in a spirit of forgiveness?

12. What does it mean to pray in a spirit of trust? Explain.

Practical Applications / Activities

1. How has this chapter helped or challenged you?

2. Reflect on / discuss gratitude, and make a list of what we often take for granted. What happens when we forget to appreciate people, things, and situations?

3. Reflect on / discuss the meaning of this statement: "Prayer is friendship with God."

4. Prayer involves not only talking to God, but also listening for God's voice. Which of these two activities seems more difficult or challenging for you, and why?

5. Recognize the importance of prayer this week. Make a specific commitment to pray. Reflect on the power of prayer. Encourage others to pray.

Prayer: *Dear God, thank you so much for your gift of prayer. We are thankful that you listen to each word we say and always respond in love. Help us appreciate the power of prayer and put it to work in our lives. May we pray in a spirit of gratitude, forgiveness, and trust, always remembering we are given the privilege of talking to Jesus. Amen.*

Chapter 8

Will You Be Remembered . . . As One Who Knew Right from Wrong?

Chapter Summary

1. Plain common sense is a good test of right and wrong.

2. Publicity is a good test of right and wrong.

3. Your best self is a good test of right and wrong.

4. Christ is a good test of right and wrong.

Reflection / Discussion Questions

1. What new insights did you receive from reading this chapter?

2. Who taught you right from wrong? Explain your learning process.

3. What particular experiences and events taught you about right and wrong?

4. In your own words, explain what having common sense means to you.

5. Give an example from your life experience of how common sense was a good test for deciding right and wrong.

6. List some reasons why "wrong" doesn't always look so bad. Give some examples.

7. Explain why "don't be silly" is often a healthy thing to say to your soul.

8. Explain the test of publicity and the rationale behind it.

9. Why is being true to yourself helpful in doing right and deciding what is right?

10. Explain the test of Christ.

11. How did one of these four tests the author lists help you make a right decision?

12. How has this discussion / reflection helped or challenged you?

Practical Applications / Activities

1. Wrong does make news. Examine a newspaper or magazine for examples of good and bad behavior.

2. List some additional tests of right and wrong.

3. List some factors that cause us to confuse right and wrong. Give some specific examples.

4. Reflect on / discuss this statement: "I often find that I have the will to do good, but not the power." How is this true in your life?

5. Pray for the wisdom to know right from wrong.

Prayer: *Dear God, you love us when we are right and when we are wrong. Thank you for loving us just the way we are. Empower us to do what is right in your eyes and to learn how to distinguish right from wrong. May we remember that all things are possible through faith and prayer. Amen.*

Chapter 9

Will You Be Remembered . . . As One Who Knew the Significance of the Battle Within?

Chapter Summary

1. We do battle within regarding how we relate to this world.

2. We do battle within regarding how we relate to other people.

3. We do battle within regarding how we relate to God and the church.

4. God loves and accepts us, just as we are.

Reflection / Discussion Questions

1. What new insights did you receive from reading this chapter?

2. In your own words, explain what is meant by "the battle within."

3. Talk about when you first realized a battle within your own life.

4. What stories in this chapter had an impact on you? Explain.

5. Why is it important to know the significance of the battle within?

6. What happened to Saul on the road to Damascus, and how does this represent the battle within?

7. What causes us to look at each day as a blessing or a grind?

8. What happens to us when we look at each day as a blessing?

9. Explain what it means that "we are accepted."

10. What causes the battle within regarding our loyalty to God and the church?

11. What are our "weapons" for fighting the battle within?

12. How has this discussion / reflection helped or challenged you?

Practical Applications / Activities

1. Watch the movie *The Natural*. Reflect on / discuss: What lessons can we learn from this movie that we can apply to our own lives?

2. Each morning, say and meditate on these words: "This is the day the LORD has made; let us rejoice and be glad in it!" (see Psalm 118:24).

3. Read and discuss the story of Saul on the road to Damascus (see Acts 9:1-20). What lessons can we learn from this story and apply to our lives?

4. Talk or write about times when you have won the battle within.

5. Reflect on / discuss how we can help others fight the battle within.

Prayer: *Dear God, there is a battle raging within each of us. Help us fight the good fight. May we remember that you love and accept us just the way we are. Your love gives us power. Thank you for all the blessings we receive from you each day. May we be appreciative for all we are given. Amen.*

Chapter 10

Will You Be Remembered . . . As One Who Knew the Power of Words?

Chapter Summary

1. We can speak the words of empathy.

2. We can speak the words of love.

3. We can speak the words of encouragement.

4. People are hungry for words that lift and heal.

Reflection / Discussion Questions

1. What new insights did you receive from reading this chapter?

2. Recall a childhood experience where you learned a lesson of the power of words.

3. What people have used words that have influenced your life? Explain.

4. Give an example of using the right words at the right moment.

5. In your own words, explain the meaning of *empathy*, and give an example.

6. What story in this chapter had an impact on you? Explain.

7. Talk about a time when words of love helped you.

8. Talk about a time when words of encouragement helped you.

9. What gives words their power?

10. Why do we remember words of love and encouragement?

11. How does the speaker benefit from speaking words of power?

12. How has this discussion / reflection helped or challenged you?

Practical Applications / Activities

1. Ask each member of the group to write words of love, empathy, or encouragement for each of the other members of the group. If persons are comfortable doing so, ask the writers to share their words aloud or distribute them on paper. You might also try this exercise with a family member or friend.

2. Create a list of positive words and phrases such as "thank you" and "I'm sorry."

3. Reflect on / discuss situations where words of empathy can help.

4. Reflect on / discuss this statement: "Say the words, and healing will come."

5. Practice saying words of empathy, love, and encouragement to people this week.

Prayer: *Dear God, your words are so powerful to us. Help us remember also that our words have an impact on others. Thank you for the gift of words and the freedom you have given us to use them. May we use words wisely. Help us speak with love in our hearts, as we are your voice to others. In Jesus' name. Amen.*

Chapter 11

Will You Be Remembered . . . As One Who Knew "That Great Gettin' Up Mornin'"?

Chapter Summary

1. Jesus wept with those he loved—and he still does.

2. Jesus raised people up—and he still does.

3. Jesus included other people in the healing process—and he still does.

4. Jesus performed no funerals, only resurrections.

Reflection / Discussion Questions

1. What new insights did you receive from reading this chapter?

2. What are your favorite songs of faith? Explain.

3. What lessons about life and God do we learn from the story of Lazarus?

4. Talk about a time when you wept with those you loved.

5. Discuss what it means to be raised up by Jesus.

6. Recall a time when you were raised up through your faith.

7. What story in this chapter had an impact on you? Explain.

8. Recall a time when you were included in the healing process.

9. Talk about an experience when people ministered to you and helped you heal.

10. When a loved one dies, in what ways do people find healing and comfort? Discuss a time when you had your faith strengthened in such a situation.

11. Who do you remember for their faith? Explain.

12. How has this discussion / reflection helped or challenged you?

Practical Applications / Activities

1. As a group or on your own, page through a hymnal and locate songs with words and phrases of hope that have a special meaning to you.

2. Discuss how weeping can be beneficial and can bring healing.

3. Use the Bible to locate stories where Jesus raised people up.

4. Reflect on / discuss this statement: "Resurrection can happen now; we don't have to wait till we die."

5. Share something you learned in this lesson with a family member or friend.

Prayer: *Dear God, thank you for the opportunity to talk about faith, and how we can be part of the healing process. Help us minister in love to friends, family, and strangers. May we speak words of love, truth, and comfort, knowing that you are with us and give us the power to do good things in your name. Amen.*

Chapter 12

Will You Be Remembered . . . As One Who Knew How to Be Beautifully Extravagant?

Chapter Summary

1. It's okay to be extravagant in our generosity.

2. It's okay to be extravagant in our gratitude.

3. It's okay to be extravagant in our graciousness.

4. The Spirit of Christ empowers us to be extravagant toward others.

Reflection / Discussion Questions

1. What new insights did you receive from reading this chapter?

2. In your own words, explain what it means to be extravagant.

3. Recall a time when you were extravagant.

4. Talk about an experience when someone was extravagant toward you.

5. What lessons do we learn from John 12:1-8, where Mary anointed Jesus' feet?

6. Recall a time when you were stingy or miserly and later regretted it.

7. What story in this chapter had an impact on you? Explain.

8. What prevents us from being extravagant sometimes?

9. Give some examples of being extravagant in gratitude.

10. Give some examples of being extravagant in graciousness or generosity.

11. Whom do you think of as being beautifully extravagant?

12. How has this discussion / reflection helped or challenged you?

Practical Applications / Activities

1. List some common examples of stingy thinking.

2. List some other areas, perhaps not mentioned in this chapter, where it is good to be extravagant.

3. Look in newspapers for examples of both beautiful extravagance and stinginess.

4. Perform an act of beautiful extravagance this week.

5. Reflect on how God has been beautifully extravagant toward you.

Prayer: *Dear God, you have richly blessed each of us. Thank you for your love and extravagance. May we be beautifully extravagant in our generosity, gratitude, and graciousness toward others. Help us remember that your love empowers us to minister to those who need assistance along life's journey. Amen.*

Chapter 13

Will You Be Remembered . . . As One Who Knew How to Be a Real Friend?

Chapter Summary

1. Friends are willing to help.

2. Friends are willing to cooperate.

3. Friends are willing to risk criticism.

4. What a friend we have in Jesus!

Reflection / Discussion Questions

1. What new insights did you receive from reading this chapter?

2. In your own words, what does it mean to be a real friend?

3. Discuss a time when someone was a real friend to you.

4. Talk about an experience where you tried to be a real friend. What were the results? How did you feel about this experience?

5. List the costs and benefits of being a real friend to others.

6. What lessons do we learn from Mark 2:1-12, where friends brought their friend to Jesus?

7. What story in this lesson had an impact on you? Explain.

8. Share how a childhood or adult friendship began.

9. List some circumstances where people especially need a friend, and what friends can do to help.

10. How does friendship benefit from—or even depend upon—a willingness to cooperate?

11. Talk about a time when you risked criticism for another person, or when another person risked criticism for you.

12. How has this discussion / reflection helped or challenged you?

Practical Applications / Activities

1. Make a list of characteristics of a real friend.

2. Locate examples in the Bible of true friendship and loyalty.

3. Start a new friendship this week, or go out of your way to help a friend.

4. Reflect on your friendship with Jesus. How might you be a better friend in this relationship?

5. Share something you learned in this lesson with a family member or friend.

Prayer: *Dear God, what a friend we have in Jesus! May we use his example to be a friend to others. Help us be open to making new friendships and allowing ourselves to be ministered to by our friends. Thank you for your love. May we love our friends just as you love us. Amen.*

Chapter 14

Will You Be Remembered . . . As One Who Knew How to Close the Gate?

Chapter Summary

1. We need to close the gate on our past successes.

2. We need to close the gate on our past hurts.

3. We need to close the gate on our past failures.

4. We all need to be set free from the tyranny of the past.

Reflection / Discussion Questions

1. What new insights did you receive from reading this chapter?

2. What does it mean to "close the gate"?

3. Why should we close the gate on our past successes?

4. Why is it sometimes hard to forget past successes? Why do we often cling to the past?

5. What is a past success that you sometimes cling to, and why?

6. What story in this chapter had an impact on you? Explain.

7. What is the reason that people remember past hurts?

8. What happens when we cling to our past hurts?

9. How are we hurt by remembering our past failures?

10. What does God want us to do with our past hurts and failures? How can God help us?

11. What is our "spiritual *delete* key," and how does—or how might—it work in your life?

12. How has this discussion / reflection helped or challenged you?

Practical Applications / Activities

1. Reflect on / discuss how we can help people recover from past hurts.

2. Reflect on things on which you need to close the gate.

3. Reflect on / talk about a time when hanging on to your past hurt your future.

4. Write out a list of your past hurts and failures, then, as a symbolic act of closing the gate on these things in your life, destroy the list. Pray, asking God to help you move on.

5. Help a friend or family member heal from a past hurt or failure. Take care not to do harm by bringing up a situation or subject that is too sensitive, or one that your friend or family member simply may not be ready to deal with at this time.

Prayer: *Dear God, our past is truly not our potential. You have great things in store for us and want us to move ahead with our lives. Help us do that and to minister to others who are held back by past hurts and failures. Thank you for your healing touch and for setting us free from our prisons. Amen.*

Epilogue: Making Every Day Count!

Epilogue Summary

1. Make every day count by being aware.

2. Make every day count by doing something good for someone else.

3. Make every day count by trusting in God for tomorrow.

4. Each day is a special gift from God.

Reflection / Discussion Questions

1. What new insights did you receive from reading this epilogue?

2. Why is it important to make every day count?

3. What prevents us from making every day count?

4. Recall a day that you made count, living to your full potential.

5. What simple things can we do to fight gloom and depression?

6. Normally, how aware are you? What things do you tend to miss?

7. What story in this lesson had an impact on you? Explain.

8. What causes us to lose our sensitivity to others and to the world?

9. Talk about a time when you did a good deed for someone or someone did a good deed for you.

10. What prevents us from trusting in God? How can we open our lives to God and become more trusting?

11. Share what you need to do more of, and what you need to do less of, in order to make each day count.

12. How has this discussion / reflection helped or challenged you?

Practical Applications / Activities

1. Reflect on / discuss how we can help others make every day count.

2. Which chapter in this book had the greatest impact on you, and why?

3. Reflect on or talk about what you learned from this book. How have you been changed?

4. Do an inventory of your life. For example, where are you in terms of reaching your goals and dreams? Which old goals or dreams do you need to let go of? What new goals and dreams have emerged, and how can you accomplish or reach them? Who are the people who matter most to you, and how is your relationship with them? Do they know how you truly feel?

5. Write down how you would like to be remembered. Include some goals or plans for how to become—or how to continue to be—this person.

Prayer: *Dear God, thank you for this time together, and for the experience that reading and studying this book has provided. We have all been greatly blessed. May we each be a more effective minister to others, sharing your love. Bless us all, and be with us as we continue life's journey. Amen.*